'Cue tape please, Ted'

An account of

MY WONDERFUL LIFE IN TELEVISION

And Radio Luxembourg

By Ted Scott.

(Up-dated 18th Sep 2018)

'Cue tape please, Ted' . . . Those four words were directed at me thousands of times. Even now, I sometimes hear them in my sleep. Oddly, I rarely did actually 'cue tape' . . . but those words formed the bedrock for the years I spent in the world of television production.

I WAS GOING TO START by telling you stories concerning The Muppets, Liberace, Bing Crosby, Bruce Forsyth, Frank Sinatra, Julie Andrews, Danny Kaye, Eddy Fisher, Bob Monkhouse, Jimi Hendrix and loads of others. Regretfully, names such as Adele, Ed Sheehan, Sam Smith, X Factor or BGT stars were all way after my time. However, the circumstances allowing me to name-drop are, to me, still unbelievable.

BACKROOM DISC CUTTING, some boot-legging, recording big bands and world famous singers, rock groups, American musical Specials, top quality dramas, sit-coms and soaps for radio and television . . . these things were not even on the outer edges of my radar in 1943. There was a war on and I was destined to be called up to fight the Japanese in some far flung corner of the world.

How did all this happen to a war-time, ill-educated, East End boy with no ambition or discernible talent and culminating in a career with a Lifetime Achievement Award? A Fellow of the *UK SCREEN AWARDS GUILD*. Wow! What would my dear old dad have made of that after bombarding me to '*get yourself a trade, son*'

There is a comprehensive index of stories to choose from ranging from '*in the beginning*' to '*the end is nigh*'
 However, if you do choose to skip through my seemingly charmed life with a near miss concerning a V2 rocket. The secrets behind programme making at Radio Luxembourg or the magic being made at the famous ATV Elstree Studios not to mention the hectic freelance world of television production, please come back and discover, among other things, how the hell I got to be Chief Engineer at Radio Luxembourg.
 I'd hate for you to miss out. But beware, it flits from one thing to another without warning!

CHAPTER HEADINGS

1. Audio-wise – in the beginning.
2. This is the army Mr Ted.
3. The bootleg escapades.
4. Radio Luxembourg the Station of the Stars.
5. Russia interferes.
6. ATV - The Light Entertainment Factory.
7. The Liberace Specials.
8. Ward 10 to Nat King Cole.
9. Sit-coms to the super Yanks.
10. Peter Pan – the 1975 version.
11. No excuses to Jimi Hendrix.
12. Some boring sound stuff.
13. Up a bit . . . fire!
14. Luxembourg ancient tid-bits.
15. And the dramas . . .
16. The Bing Crosby Shows.
17. Julie's Favourite Things.
18. The Muppet Years.
19. More ATV memories.
20. The freelance world.
21. Limehouse TV – Canary Wharf.
22. Bob Hope – lost in space!
23. Paul Daniels to Birds of a Feather.
24. Dallas to Israel via Bergen.
25. The end is nigh . . .
26. Gordon Bennett – How the rich live.

1. In the beginning . . . audio-wise.

I STARTED WORK AT 14 after being evacuated three times. This involved attending several different schools in a war-time environment. My father wanted me to be a mechanic; *'Get yourself a trade, boy'* was his doctrine. I had no clue about a career path. I had dreams, a musician perhaps? Just how difficult could it be to learn an instrument?

On leaving school dad found me a minor office job in a cable manufacturing company in Lea Bridge Road, Leyton, E10. I started at 8am and spent most of the day getting teas and sandwiches from a mobile catering truck outside the building for what seemed like a multitude of starving office workers. I magnified the awfulness to my ever attentive dad, thus my first job had lasted one day.

Still harping on about a trade, he found me work in a small garage in Wanstead. I barely lasted a week. The briefness of my stay being exacerbated by crossing the thread while changing a spark plug on the Guvnor's Jaguar SS. So that temporarily put paid to dad's mechanical aspirations for me. Another career he envisioned for me involved the retail trade at Messrs. Dunne & Co (*if you want to get ahead – get a hat*) a posh shop in Leytonstone High Street. I failed the dress code requirements when a bowler hatted area manager showed up after three days.

You perceive how easy it was in those days to get employment. No diplomas, no A or O levels . . . they hadn't been invented yet. Even during, and shortly after, the war I'm pretty sure the general education system was considerably better than later curriculums.

These days, a number of 'A' levels and even a spell at a university often doesn't guarantee you much more than a minimum wage and that will be after a gruelling series of interviews on the telephone, or skype. Or, eventually if you're lucky, a personal interview.

Perhaps I could be something in the city? Dad then found me an office job (post boy) in the shipping world of Leadenhall Street. *United States Lines* (provider of Liberty Ships) was situated at 38 Leadenhall Street. EC1. Their ocean liner 'United States' still holds the Blue Rib and for the fastest transatlantic crossing.

Although an American company it was staffed by stiff upper lipped British executives. The ferocious Mr. H. E. Walker in pin-striped trousers and black morning coat easily earned the nick-named 'high explosive' in those wartime days. With smarmed back hair and a military moustache, Mr. Chambers (finance director) similarly garbed would loudly yell *'COME'* when a knock at his door dared to infringe on his space.

Office manager Mr Bell condescended to see my father speaking on my behalf for a position. What would I have done without dad? My slight stammer increased at times of stress almost disappearing later (I liked to think!). *The U.S Lines* Managing Director, Clinton Hiram Kemp, always in a light grey lounge suit, mysteriously came and went with a briefcase chained to his wrist. Was he CIA? Did the CIA exist then? When a liberty ship went down, the 'Bill of Lading' was transferred from the vault to the 'dead room'. *US Lines* telephone number was Royal 6677. Funny, I remember it to this day, while not sure of my own mobile number.

In London at that time day-time air raids were still common and we had afire watch duty roster, involving a trip to the fifth floor rooftop. If an enemy plane was spotted approaching, an alarm bell was activated and the staff would scurry down to the basement (hastily followed by the bell ringer).

If after ten minutes, or so, nothing happened, both fire-watcher and office workers would drift back to their desks. Nobody appeared too bothered, it was a common event. Exciting at first, boring later. A skylight on the roof gave access to the telephone room where the office girls would meet for morning coffee. These conflabs, involving much giggling, intrigued me and, although I couldn't see them, I could vaguely hear the girls through a hole in the window frame woodwork.

Borrowing a large funnel from mum's kitchen I jammed the pointed end into the woodwork and was able to discern the girls through the horn end. I liked to think that this was my first venture into sound amplification!

The voluptuous Miss Gray (a dead ringer for Jane Russell) told stories about how her GI boyfriend couldn't keep his hands off her, whilst a stunning beauty, Miss McDougal related tips on how to juggle two GI boyfriends and her Scots Guards fiancée. His name was Hamish. Even today, whenever this name crops up, Miss McDougal's image comes to mind. When Miss McDougal walked down Leadenhall Street, lamp posts would wince as gentlemen usually walked into them.

I had no experience of grown up girls before and it was all heady stuff for a fourteen year old and my blood temperature often soared. Once, on fire watch duty I was so engrossed I totally missed a Heinkel bomber passing over. Of course, when the girls got back to their desks, butter wouldn't melt.

The journey to the City from Leytonstone was forty minutes, or so, by bus. This journey gave an opportunity to observe any bomb damage either from the night before or even during the day. One would discover the odd shop no longer standing and lots of broken windows. Homeward bound, often more carnage would be seen. Would my house still be standing? With no means of communication with home, this would be incomprehensible today.

When dad was invalided out of the army in early 1942, I reluctantly left the possibility of becoming a shipping magnate to help dad, who had found an empty shop adjoining the newly built Rex cinema in Leytonstone High Road, E11. He had the idea of opening a coffee bar. Very innovative at that time. He and mum had no previous catering experience but mum was a terrific cook and dad always had entrepreneurial leanings (often falling over!).

Before the war, after serving seven years in the peace-time army, dad was a meter reader/emptier. Heavy bags of old pennies were the order of the day back then and dad covered the East End boroughs of Aldgate, Mile End and Bow, where he claimed he emptied the meters in every house. He often said we would be appalled at the way poor people lived in those hovels in the thirties. You'd be appalled now, dad, to know those 'hovels' sell now for over a quarter of a million pounds. I know of a television script writer who bought a terraced house in Tredegar Square, Bow, for well over half a million pounds, and that was in the eighties!

With three young kids and pushing forty, being called up in 1940 to serve King and Country was not dad's idea of fair play, but called up he was. The Royal Corps of Signals was his destination. Considering his credentials, the unlikeliest branch of the armed forces possible. He ended up at a 'secret' house in Beckenham near London making tea for a cacophony of clever (and apparently, beautiful) ATS girls and cypher clerks, while we spent our nights in an air raid shelter in the back garden of Grove Road, Leytonstone. This became a ritual. The air raid siren would go around tea-time. Down to the shelter with a flask and perhaps bread and jam. Lots of ack-ack guns, the occasional bomb going on and then the all clear around dawn.

A word here for the outstanding organizational skills of our Government at that time. Months before war was declared, virtually every garden in suburban London had an air raid *Anderson* shelter installed by local council workers. Those without a garden got a *Morrison* shelter, a heavily reinforced dining table with metal sides that could withstand bomb damage after a direct hit.

Underground stations were being transformed to take people sheltering from possible air raids. I doubt whether the red-tape thinking that exists today could have come anywhere close to that achievement. While we're at it, those skills at organizing the evacuation of well over a million London kids would baffle the present regime with red tape and health and safety issues.

I haven't a clue as to why dad thought catering was his metier. Anyway, with minimum funding we got stuck in at the empty shop next to the virtually new Rex Cinema and eventually **Scott's Buffet** was born. We worked all night for (what seemed like) weeks decorating, making and fitting counters and generally getting ready for the launch.

Now that air raids were getting less frequent a huge window was installed without shatter glass strips. An innovation at that time. One morning, just minutes after I cleaned this beautiful brand new window a V2 rocket fell nine hundred yards away and blew the entire window outwards. It was a massive explosion. Furniture and the floor in the buffet shook. It sounded like something had landed next door.

The brand new shop window had been sucked outwards by the explosion. Huge shards of dangerous glass were blown across the road towards the pub opposite. Luckily, no-one was passing although I think a bus got a few shards in the side. The pub opposite had no damage at all, no glass broken . . . my charmed life had begun.

The buffet was a great success and became a haven of rest for American Air Force personnel, many of which were stationed close by, thanks largely to mum's superb coffee and cuisine, which she insisted had to be of the standard as if feeding her own family.

Being close to the Burghley Hall, a popular dance hall hot spot of the time, the alternating bands would spend their break times in Scott's Buffet and in one of these breaks I fortuitously met boy wonder drummer Kenny Clare, later to be voted second best drummer in the world by Metronome Magazine (it was always difficult to top Buddy Rich). Kenny lived in Richmond Road, Leytonstone. His dad, Norman, was also a drummer but more in the style of Victor Sylvester. Watch Kenny in action, soloing on Kenny Clarke Big Band link on YouTube.

From around the age of 12, I did two morning paper rounds. This gave the chance to be first on the scene to find fresh chunks of shrapnel, often still warm from the air raids the night before. I once found a whole incendiary bomb. Regretfully (or luckily) a copper saw me with it and relieved me of my treasure.

I also did a Hitchman's Dairies milk round on Saturday mornings with horse and cart. The milkman was a 'milk-lady', unusual in those days. Saturday was pay-the-bill day and we rarely finished until 4.30 pm when, after stabling the horse, she took me to her house where her disabled husband used to make a special tea with cream cakes, a treat in those days. I relish the thoughts of those Saturdays, even now.

In retrospect, I'm sure that meeting Kenny Clare gave me the impetus to try and emulate him (fat chance). The proceeds from my part-time jobs enabled me to purchase a second-hand John Grey drum kit. I think it cost £40 and consisted of bass drum, snare, hi-hat and a Zildjian cymbal on a chrome stand. The Zildjian was a remarkable find, probably worth more than the rest of the kit. They aren't much used these days because having been hit they 'rang' for ages. You may see (and hear) those at the Albert Hall played by one of several percussionists. Notice the way they immediately dampen it down as soon as they have struck the cymbals together. The modern crash cymbal is more suitable to present day musical needs and the Zildjian now has several versions of that. Had I hit *my* Zildjian with any strength with drum sticks, the resulting sound would have frightened all the dancers on the floor of the *Cock Hotel* in Chingford High Street where I gigged. Only wire brushes could be used.

Joe Morello the drummer with the Dave Brubeck Quartet was a master of the brushes. On the *Dave Digs Disney* album, he takes a sixty four bar solo using just brushes. Fantastic. This album, together with *Jazz at Oberlin* is vital to own for any Brubeck fan. Both are beautifully recorded. Many years later, I had the pleasure of talking to Joe, who was virtually blind, pointing out where his drum mikes were when they played *Sunday Night at the London Palladium.*

By listening avidly to my dozen, or so, favourite jazz records, I could 'play' drums to my heart's content on the kitchen table - but not quite so easily on an actual drum kit. Practise, practise helped, despite mum and dad (and a neighbour, or two) suffering the thuds and crashes of paradiddles seeping from my bedroom door, which barely now had room for a bed!

I was lucky enough to meet George Sims, who lived at the top of my road in Leytonstone above a bank (possibly Barclays). George, who was quite old (about 38) had a group called *The Blue Jays.* His drummer, an extremely old gentleman (pushing fifty!) was no longer able to travel. I have no knowledge how George found out I played drums. Surely my practising didn't leak that far afield? Anyway, I got the gig and found myself working every weekend. My role in the group was to keep tempo with the minimum of noise. No Gene Krupa histrionics, even if I were capable of such.

The *Cock Hotel* in Chingford High Street had a small ballroom which was well attended. The *Blue Jay's* repertoire went from old fashioned waltz to a heady quickstep with an occasional foray into the Hokey Cokey. George doubled alto saxophone and violin. He had a small car which only had room for George and the pianist. The bass player had transport but he lived miles away. Thus, I had to make my own way on public transport although George Sims eventually relented and fitted my gear in his teensy boot. But once or twice I did use public transport to get to and from Chingford. Sometimes carrying my kit home from the Green Man bus depot in Leytonstone close to my house.

By this time, air raids were rare although the anti-aircraft guns on the Wanstead flats often hammered at unseen German airplanes. They made more noise than any falling bombs. Later, when V1's and V2's entered the conflict, ack-ack guns were of little use.

For those not afflicted with the old age label, it may be advantageous to explain V1's and V2's. By the time the Germans were unable to launch further serious air raids their scientists had developed the V1 bomb. Smaller than a fighter plane, the 1000 lb bomb had wings and a form of propulsion on the tail giving it great speed and a distinctive noise.

They were launched from France with just enough fuel to expire over London. When the 'distinctive noise' stopped, you waited with baited breath for the explosion that followed some thirty seconds later. The RAF Spitfires, barely able to match their speed, often dived alongside as they crossed the English Channel to tip their wings putting them off course. Many crashed into the sea.

I was friendly with the projector operators at the Rex cinema next to the buffet. One evening, on the roof, we actually saw a V1 passing about 1000 yards away BELOW the level of the Rex. Wow! It went on for ages never to explode in our neck of the woods.

The V2 was a more advanced animal; a huge rocket that gave no warning of its approach. A fore-runner of the intercontinental ballistic missile. After several mysterious explosions it was announced that they were gas mains exploding. Until we all worked out that there couldn't be that many gas main explosions.

Standing at a Harrow Green bus stop in Leytonstone one bright sunny morning, a huge bang made us all look upwards to discover that a V2 had prematurely exploded a mile, or so, above us. The more diligent observer hastily sought shelter in a shop doorway to escape falling shrapnel.

Incidentally, the V2 that destroyed the window of *Scott's Buffet* minutes after I cleaned it, landed some half a mile away in Barclay Road, almost opposite the Burghley Hall where Kenny Clare played and close to Leytonstone church. I visited the scene shortly after and saw a dead horse with an up-turned milk float. That image remains with me despite the row of demolished houses and subsequent loss of life.

I remember my mum out shopping in Leytonstone one bright morning when a Messerschmitt 109 strafed the High Street. The church suffered bullet holes in its outer wall.

After the war, the ascendancy of American rocketry was largely due to the 'liberated' German scientists. Its mind blowing to think that had the war lasted another year, they would have mastered the production of the atom bomb. Imagine one falling on a British city like Hull or Bristol. Capitulation would have been a certainty.

Leadenhall Street, the hub of the shipping industries offices was virtually unscathed by bombs and rockets, although in the early hours of one winter morning, a patrolling bobby had his helmet knocked off by an unseen landmine, the parachute of which had got caught in the Cunard Building flag-poles. A landmine was a block of 1000 lb-plus explosive. After groping around in the dark for his helmet, and seeing the monster chunk of steel still swaying, the copper called the bomb disposal squad.

Was there a braver bunch of people than the bomb disposal squad?

The Rex Cinema next to Scott's Buffet had two giant collection boxes in the foyer. They invited patrons to contribute towards the cost of aeroplanes to assist in the destruction of the Axis regime. Apparently, £5000 would secure the building of a Spitfire fighter plane whilst £25,000 was the cost of a Lancaster bomber. This Government sponsored charity appeal was countrywide and raised many millions of pounds towards the war effort. The Battle of Britain was much heralded with great visual posters to accompany the appeal. A marvellous piece of propaganda. My dear old dad always maintained that when it came to propaganda, we had Dr. Gobbels was well and truly snookered.

My father eventually put his foot down and stopped me from gigging while air raids were happening. Having miniscule doubts as to my expertise, I reluctantly put the drum kit away. It was time to experiment with a freshly purchased clarinet and later a second-hand, slightly battered trombone, it was £12, I think, from a pawn broker in Leyton. You had to blow into it a certain way to produce a note. Then find the slide position to change that certain note. The slide had about seven positions and there were even slide positions between those.

Most instruments give you a planned note when activated, such as the piano or vibraphone etc. The trombone, like the trumpet family relied upon embouchure to strike the right note. It was all rather confusing, especially when you weren't too sure what the word embouchure meant! Perhaps proper tutorship, preferably from a very early age, would have helped, or more likely, I just didn't 'have it'.

Anyway, my plan to be a musician turned out to be a pipe dream, about the only thing I could actually play apart from the drum kit, which now got a resurgence. I sold the Zildjian cymbal and got two crash cymbals a small tom tom and still had a couple of quid over.

The Gene Krupa records came out again and I played along with him in my little bedroom. Mum and dad were ecstatic! With the war still ongoing and other boys were planning to join the army it seems pretty stupid now that I was so fixated on a career I had no obvious talent for. My massive interest in music must have been influential. Not just modern jazz either. I was a BBC Home Service fan as well. The music of Eric Coates and other mainstream composers also interested me.

The Saturday morning broadcasts of the Bernie Braden Show with the Sid Philips Orchestra was a programme I never missed. Classical music I also listened to but couldn't come to terms with chamber music – still can't. But surely I could be a part of this world? The easiest route seemed to be by playing an instrument. But those I tried were woefully unsuccessful.

For all my dalliances with instruments, dad would still shake his head; *'You should have learnt a trade, boy'.* Mum and dad always called me boy. I detested my given name Walter, choosing a middle name, first Charles then Edward, shortened sometimes to Ed, Eddie, or Ted. No wonder they got confused and kept to boy?

It's 1945. The war against the axis had ended. The Buffet had been sold and dad had moved on to another catering outlet, then another. I had little choice but to stay in the catering trade where I either skivvied in the kitchen or hob-knobbed with the clientele. At one point dad bought a very fancy ice cream cart which he parked outside the latest café. I became the cornet filler.

Mum was still head cook while dad retained his ability to cut ham so thin you could see through it. His customer relations exercise took a hammering when, for a joke, he told customers that Alec Bedser had dropped dead at the wicket during the latest test match. It put many off their lunch and even caused a temporary boycott. This dreary routine continued for two years until approaching eighteen years of age, the magic number occurred where National

Service loomed. Not a heady prospect. The future looks gloomy.

***

2. This is the army Mr Ted . . .

1947. WITH THE WAR IN EUROPE done and dusted, National Service would have entailed a boat trip to the Far East to join in the fight against the Japanese. However, Hiroshima and Nagasaki put paid to that prospect. My call-up papers arrived and within weeks I am invited to attend Canterbury Barracks.

Kenny Clare and Dennis Sullivan, my two closest friends, came to see me off from Victoria Station where I was en route to the BUFFS Barracks for six weeks basic training. Kenny and Dennis are trying hard not to snigger at my haircut. My long, golden locks had been given the elbow. Rather than let the army butcher have a go, I had a crew cut at my local hairdressers.

Within months of waving goodbye, both of my sniggering mates would be called up in the RAF, Their crew cuts, performed by the Company barber, were infinitely funnier than mine. Kenny continued his drumming career in the Royal Air Force dance band, a very professional outfit while Dennis worked his way around various RAF establishments with the same aplomb he employed with his skill at ballroom dancing. How we envied him. Dance halls were feeding ground for boys seeking girls. Kenny was very girl-shy, I was no better. Instead of learning to cut the light fantastique, we sat on long bus journeys from Leytonstone to Dagenham and back counting bars in our head to see how close we got to each other.

For the aficionados, counting sixty four bars in your head at foxtrot tempo and getting within a couple of seconds of each other was considered top marks. Maintaining a steady rhythm was essential even for the basic drummer. Setting different tempos, samba and quickstep etc....more tricky.

My small suitcase en route to Canterbury contained two 78 rpm records; Woody Herman's *Apple Honey* and Stan Kenton's *Artistry In Rhythm*, both presents from Kenny as my copies had worn so thin the track on the 'B side' could almost be heard. Woody didn't make Canterbury but Stan lasted out thousands of miles.

The BUFFS (Third Regiment of Foot) were the oldest infantry regiment dating back to 1572 and renowned for their valour, hence the saying; *'Steady the Buffs'*. Our quietly spoken drill sergeant assured us that despite looking like a bunch of poofs, in six weeks we would not know ourselves.

He was true to his word, we doubled everywhere, backwards and forwards to the parade ground, to the latrines at 6 am and to the canteen with knife, fork and spoon clasped behind our back (fork prongs facing outwards lest we should stumble and accidentally stab ourselves).

After the arduous training most of us freely admitted we never felt better. I wasn't keen on becoming a 'regiment of foot' person. After occasional confusing my right foot from my left, together with a dismal record on the rifle range, there were some doubts as to my qualifications to become an infantryman. These doubts were added to when my slight stammer limited my ability to coherently shout *'Halt, who goes there?'* in a commanding fashion. The quietly spoken drill sergeant pointed out (to the amusement of my platoon) that by the time I questioned the intruder, I would have a bayonet in my gullet.

After basic training, I was confirmed to be non-infantry material and posted to the Royal Army Service Corps stronghold at Farnborough to take a course in shorthand writing. Followers of the perversities of military procedure will not be amazed to learn that, despite the twelve weeks course and achieving a modicum of success in both shorthand and typing, I was NEVER ever required to perform either task. There were anomalies; if you 'volunteered' to drive a tank thinking you'd be doing some cushy office job, don't bank on it. You may well end up driving a tank!

The guard duties were arduous; it took an hour to get prepared lots of *'blanco-ing'* and polishing. The guard commanders could discover a minute flaw in your appearance at twenty paces incurring dreadful penalties. Sitting on our beds awaiting the call one Saturday afternoon we were disturbed by a harrowed second lieutenant bursting into our hut;

'Anyone here name Scott?'

'Yes sir, here' I replied.

'Got you down in your pay book as a drummer dance band – right?'

'Right . . . sir'

'Come with me Scott, you're playing tonight in the Sergeant's Mess'

I pointed out that it was impossible as I was on guard shortly. This was pooh poohed with a wave of the hand. We walked briskly to the camp hall.

'What's your name Scott – first name?'

'Ted, sir'

'Well, Ted our regular drummer is George Scott, any relation?'

'No sir'

'Unfortunately he's had to go on compassionate leave, could be quite a while it seems, the band is waiting to give you a bit of a rehearsal'.

The band was an eighteen-piece affair, a bit different from George Sims and the *Blue Jays* that I had been used to. These were proper musicians, many of them later to appear in top British bands. A super Premier kit awaited complete with three tom toms, a proper hi-hat and three crash cymbals.

It was stuff beyond my wildest dreams and experience. Drum music stared at me, I could just about read but not sight read. I explained this to them and they seemed quite unperturbed. Luckily they started off with Glenn Miller's American Patrol. I knew this piece backwards, even the four bar Buddy Rich drum solo towards the end which being quite simple (for Buddy) I achieved without mishap. Luckily also, I knew most of their book. You don't get to listen to jazz records until they wore thin without being able to 'play' them in your sleep. Okay, I made a few mistakes but I figure they were accepted as the other option was no drummer at all.

Drumming was different in those days. You worked the hi-hat and bass drum to attain tempo with the odd tickle on the snare drum. The drum sticks were held in a strict fashion, not un-like a knife and fork. Today, sticks are held like battering rams and flash around the kit, often at breakneck speed. How wonderful it would have been if I could play like the DIRE STRAIGHTS drummer . . . but then, his kit would have seeped out of my bedroom, across the landing and into mum and dad's bedroom.

Sensibly I soon learned that keeping it simple (and quiet) was better than making a twit of myself attempting too much. The 'proper' musicians in the band probably found it easier on the ear also.

In the ensuing weeks I often spent a few hours in the dance band Nissen hut where they lived a different life from us squaddies. Posters of pin-up girls plastered the walls and (astoundingly) beds left un-made. It was great to be a musician in the forces, or a sportsman. It was a life I could certainly get used to. But, let's face it, I was woefully out-classed. George Scott was due back shortly (almost certainly to everyone's relief) and my future life in the army was changed when one of the trombone players whose day-time job in the postings department asked;

'Hey, Ted, how would you like a posting to London? They want a technical mechanist clerk at the RASC depot, White City'.

I jumped at it. Being on the Central Line I could get the underground direct to Leytonstone, and home. The RASC depot was virtually on the site where the BBC Television Centre stood at White City. My task there was mostly paperwork, booking out spare parts for army vehicles, but more importantly, lighting the stove in the CO's office before he turned up for work. This was the winter of 1947, the worst winter in memory. Oh how I tried to keep that fire going before he arrived. His glowering disappointment finally prompted the question;

'What did you do in civvy street, Scott?'
'I was a drummer, sir'
He is perplexed; 'What a door-to-door salesman?'
'No sir, dance band'
'Dance band?' he winced.

That didn't figure in his sphere of social life, but he is now beginning to comprehend how the stove lighting task is beyond my ken. Within three weeks, I am posted to Thetford in Norfolk. This is an embarkation camp where life is made a little 'unpleasant' so that when you are eventually posted to some foreign clime you will be rather chuffed to leave. Shortly before I got to Thetford, two squaddies had hung themselves in the toilets.

My posting came after two weeks in a freezing cold environment with endless parades to either have your posting read out, or much worse, your menial task for the rest of the dismal day. Painting trees trunks brown or inexplicably painting a mountain of coal white at the rear of the cookhouse was not high on the list of sensible things to be doing, especially in the infamous 1947 winter of

discontent. Then one morning the duty sergeant yells out my name;
'1918445 Private Scott...embarking to the Middle East for onward posting. Get your kit ready, embarking in thirty six hours".

The Middle East! Surely not. Someone had previously whispered that a military shorthand writer was wanted in New York; just up my street, I thought. Transpired to be a vicious rumour. Given twelve hours leave, I just had time to go home and say goodbye to mum and my sisters. By now they were ensconced in a café in Station Road, Manor Park. Dad was out doing a deal!

After a convoluted train journey from Norwich to Liverpool via London, we embarked on the *SS Scythia* - a troopship leftover from the war. She was a single stack ex-liner from the *White Star Line*. Having never been more than twenty miles from home I was strangely excited. On the third morning at sea on deck watching the coast of Portugal float by, twinkling lights from houses on the mountainside could be seen, the winter of discontent left far behind. A different world indeed.

Later we are in Gibraltar, then Malta, then Port Said, our final destination before *SS Scythia* steamed on to Singapore. The food on the ship is first class. The bread freshly made every day. For us squaddies, more accustomed to wartime rationing, it is the height of luxury. The Captain gave us lectures. Apparently, this ship was used to transport Russians back from prisoner of war camps to Murmansk. He recounted how, when queuing for their food, they put the soup, the main course and the pudding all on one plate, mixed it up and consumed it with great relish.

This and other tales left us eighteen-year-olds in awe. But not as much awe as we discovered in Port Said. On docking, there were little boys diving under the huge ship to recover coins thrown in. Ashore, other little boys offered to introduce you to their sister. Even more little boys were keen to clean your boots. A refusal incurred much bad language (in English) and a dollop of something awful on your boots, now in dire need of a clean.

An open-air cinema was situated in the backyards of blocks of flats. Washing hanging from windows partially obscured the screen showing a film with four lots of subtitles over it. Nobody listened to the sound track and several other little boys constantly buzzed around selling various wares in, what seemed like, two or three languages. King Farouk's image and the National Anthem at the end of the programme brought sudden silence everywhere. To attempt to exit during this was inadvisable.

After a week in Port Said, we are transported by train to Port Suez, some eighty miles of crawling along with the canal on one side and endless sand dunes on the other. On the train another little boy, dressed in his nightshirt, traverses the corridor selling bars of chocolate from a tray around his neck. He is barely ten and cheerfully doing good business when an Egyptian military policeman grabs him by the collar, opens the carriage door and chucks him out. It's all desert out there, the occasional hut or donkey. We watch in horror as he picks himself up, retrieves his tray and what few piastres he has accumulated and casually wanders off amidst those endless sand dunes. Life is cheap here, I hope it has changed in sixty years, but I doubt it.

The transit camp at Port Suez is huge. There are rows and rows of tents interspersed with seemingly dozens of shops owned by the locals. Every third one is a 'dhobi wallah' offering a superb uniform clean and press service for a pittance. In twenty odd months in the Middle East those 'dhobi wallahs' kept us looking smart at all times.

The vast camp is occupied by an assortment of regiments from Scots Guards to Welsh Fusiliers, all awaiting postings. The NAAFI at night is a dynamite keg waiting to be lit by copious quantities of alcohol. One night, while on perimeter guard duty, I and a couple of others are diverted to attend a commotion in the NAAFI. It appears a rather large Irish gentleman had smashed a few tables over another gentleman's heads and, on being requested by the Orderly Officer of the night to stop mucking about, he punches the said officer in the snout.

Now, if you offend the Orderly Officer, whatever his rank, you have offended the ultimate Camp Commander – who was, I believe a Lt-Colonel. The rather large Irish gentleman in question, now overcome by quantities of guards, is stripped naked and chained to a bed in the guardhouse. I believe he got seven years. No time off for good behaviour but time added for bad. Life was cheap in the British Armed Forces. I hope it has changed in sixty-plus years!

I remember two Scottish chaps in our tent always helping themselves to our cigarette rations in almost incomprehensible Glaswegian. Once (after yet another heavy night in the NAAFI) they decided on a lay-in. A sergeant inspecting the tents at 7.30 am for malingerers found them a'slumber. He woke them by prodding the inert bodies with his stick and they showed their joint annoyance by biffing him, laying him out cold. They got three years – sergeants obviously not being as offended by a bout of fisticuffs as Orderly Officers.

My group of mates dwindled as postings came through for Mombasa, Aden and all points east. Finally, the last fifteen of us are told to report to the ferry to take us across the canal where we were to board another train headed for Palestine. The journey takes two days after occasionally being slowed by a sapper walking in front of the train with a mine detector.

On this journey, I meet some guy who recounts to me his life in Civvy Street. He owns two houses, a motor car, a boat on the Thames and boasts a half dozen girlfriends – yet he has never done a day's work in his life. He is looking forward to Palestine, where (he proclaims) a possible fortune can be made. Is he having me on with these tales? For fifteen hours in the slow moving train he relates his life story, no doubt considerably embellish.

(I store his tales and use them many years later in a trilogy of fiction books. I changed his name to Gordon Bennett. I barely remember his actual name, even if it were real).

In the army, most of the idle talk is about girls left behind. In point of fact, very few had 'girls left behind' - boasting of female conquests was par for the course. I only ever had one (rather part-time) 'girl left behind' a blonde stunner named Barbara Rogers from Leyton. What larks in her doorway having been to the flicks, hoping her dad didn't suddenly appear! She promised to write to me but never did.

Haifa. It's December 1947; British troops have left in droves. As Jewish refugees flood in, Palestinian homes are being confiscated and not surprisingly, there is a general air of discontent. We brave fifteen, freshly arrived are now ensconced in an army camp on Mount Sinai. The camp used to hold hundreds but they have vamoosed. Every afternoon a train chugs by below us on the mountain and fires machine guns into the sea. No rhyme or reason but our first experience of hearing real guns since joining up.

Rather bored, some of us decided to wander down into town and see what's going on. The duty sergeant wouldn't let us out unarmed. However, he further told us 'they' would not hesitate to chop your arm off to get at your rifle. We decided to play cards instead and generally enhance tales of our previous female conquests.

After three weeks of inactivity, one sunny morning we are bundled into a K5 Austin 3-ton truck heading for Haifa docks. En route, the same duty sergeant advised;
'Keep your heads down chaps - a lot of stray bullets about.' We board a small steamer (about 5000 tons) with a hundred or so Cypriot troops. Our destination is Cyprus. En route, the weather is atrocious with frightening

thunderstorms, sheet lightning and heaving seas. Life below decks is not a runner what with the smell and inert Cypriot soldiers. Up top, there are more dreadfully ill Cypriot soldiers, some may have even got washed overboard – who knows?

Next morning, drained of all life on the sick infested deck, we awake to sunshine and calmness with the coast of Cyprus looming up. Sunshine and calmness combined with peace and tranquillity sums up my twenty months of army life on that beautiful island.

On disembarking, fourteen of, what are now, my closest pals, are taken to 695 Company outside the port of Famagusta in northern Cyprus. I alone am decreed to join 471 Company in Nicosia. Life is cruel it appears. Not for me however, 471 Company was a doddle posting whilst 695 Company was Aldershot and Farnborough combined in the blistering sun.

471 Company, Nicosia, is a Royal Army Service Corps camp positioned in a small wood. Trucks from all over Cyprus come here for repairs. The mechanics are Cypriot, or Turkish or even Armenian. There is very little dissent. That was to come years later. About twenty of us lived in a Nissen hut (on site) in some degree of comfort. It wasn't Butlins to be sure but I had landed on my feet.

I worked in a small wooden hut issuing chits to mechanics to obtain spare parts. On one occasion I felt something on my feet. I looked below my desk and, to my horror, saw a snake crawling over my boots. Must have eight foot long and quite fat. I broke land speed records for exiting the office.

A couple of Cypriot mechanics heard my scream, came running and manhandled the snake out. Later it was cooked on an open fire and I was offered first slice. Being a jellied ell fanatic, I dug in. Wasn't bad.

My musical 'talents' were later gleaned from my trusty pay book and I was recruited to play at various army venues in a small combo more suited to my drumming abilities. We got ten shillings a gig, apparently musician union rules! That's odd; I never got a penny from the big band at Farnborough! It probably went to that George Scott!

I had been promoted to corporal by this time – war substantiated no less. This meant that in the event of a war, I could return to that rank. Golly, can't wait for that!

The Commanding Officer of 471 RASC Company discovered that in Civvy Street I had looked after my father's books. The café business in those days with rationing was a minefield of paperwork. The Captain enquired whether I could 'look at' his personal books. I did. He had several investments and I assisted with his tax returns. You will perceive this was a very laid-back, cushy posting.

The beautifully spoken Captain, not much older than me, always called me *'Mr. Ted'*. Later in life, Keith Beckett, the television director on the Val Doonican series always addressed me as *'Mr. Ted'*.

I learnt to drive at that camp. On weekends, we would scoot around the tree infested camp in whatever transport we could find. I seriously crunched a Humber Super Snipe (top officer's wheels) causing damage to the bonnet, bumper and a wing. Two Cypriot mechanics were rounded up and they repaired the damage before the Monday morning roll call.

The Berlin airlift was happening around this time and we were all given another three months added to our two years National Service. Cyprus is only a hundred miles or so from Russian soil and some top brass hat must have considered an invasion a possibility.

This hypothesis never touched the busy cafes and bars of delightful Metaxas Square in Nicosia. Life went on as usual and peace reigned. However, one night we were awakened by the roar of a motor cycle within the confines of our Nissen hut. It was four am.

One of the guys, John Preston, was a motorcycle nut. He had entered for the all Middle East championships and won first prize. A huge gold cup. He and his fellow motorcycle compatriots had gone out to Nicosia to celebrate and on returning, John had wheeled his machine into the hut and started it up with crazy revving. Apparently he wanted to inform us of his victory. We got the message, he was chuffed. Apart from that, it was quiet on the Cyprus front.

During my stay a lance corporal had been found stealing from our lockers in the Nissen hut. He was found guilty and sentence to three years in a detention centre in Port Said. Being a Corporal it necessitated two of similar rank to accompany him on the journey via ship. It's me and another guy.

Chained to our wrists, the three of us arrive in Port Said and report to the guard commander at the gate. Inside, the floors are like mirrors[i] and the whole place reeks of discipline multiplied by a hundred. We stand in front of a Military Police Officer while the guard commander prods the culprit to answer questions from the quietly spoken MP Officer a millisecond after being asked. Boy, were we glad to be out of that environment. Once more, no time off for good behaviour but time added for bad.

Eventually, demob loomed up. It's 1949. A flight to Tobruk in an ancient Dakota gave the chance to view from above lots of sunken ships in the harbour, still lying there awaiting salvage. A scrap dealers dream. Venturing inland was verboten, lots of hidden land mines. A stroll on the beach revealed a rusting German U Boat washed up. The periscope had long been purloined but entry into the dark monster was frighteningly inhibiting. Ten days later, we board the troopship, *Empress of Australia* (21,800 tons) for the journey home. Yippee, take me back to dear old *blighty*. On disembarkation in Liverpool I am given a demob suit, but choose to wear my dhobied, sun-dyed, khaki with white lanyard with multiple Middle East flashes.

My sun-tan, which we all took for granted, drew looks of envy.

On hitting London, I traverse the Central Line to eventually meet up with mum and dad. On the tube I sit alongside rows of dismal-looking people, all in dire need of some sun. *Blighty* aint looking so hot. Mum and dad greet me, taking me to their latest venture, a huge transport café on the old Southend Road (the *Ace of Hearts*) with a cottage alongside for the family.

A transport café is no picnic. Lyons Corner House, it aint! Mum is cooking 100 plus lunches a day for burly drivers as if they were her own family. Business is VERY brisk. I have become the champion chip maker in Essex. Cindy, my youngest sister was still at school, the two older girls, Sylvia and Jean, work behind the counter, mum is head cook while I am taking the place of a domestic dish washer which, apparently, hasn't been invented yet. Dad is 'client relations' – which means he does very little.

Some months later I am peeling sack-loads of potatoes on my twenty-first birthday awaiting the rush of coach parties returning from enjoying the annual Southend Lights extravaganza.

Rather like Blackpool, but not quite as grand, Southend is the mecca for the majority of East London inhabitants. Coach loads of punters traversed the old Southend Road where dad craftily gave the coach drivers a crisp one pound note and free tea and buns whenever they pulled in. The best customers in the world are the 'poorer' type of customer. Out to enjoy themselves, money is no object. These coach trips were great business.

We work all day for the transport lorry drivers, then until past midnight for the returning coach loads of punters.

Cyprus, beautiful Cyprus, the biblical Jewel of the Mediterranean, is a distant memory. Life looks bleak. What the hell am I going to do?

***

3. The bootleg escapade . . .

HAVING NOW MOVED from café to café several times, mum and dad found the work tiring. Sixteen hour days were par for the course and it was no life for me or my sisters. Dad vainly sought alternative means of a living before finishing up in a failing office furniture business. To facilitate this meant us having to move house so many times, I cannot catalogue locations with any certainty. Dad's exploits and hard work in trying to avoid 'hard work' would fill a book.

Kenny Clare had served his National Service in the RAF and we had always kept in touch. One weekend I stayed with Kenny and told him the future looked bleak, I might have to actually find a job! After much speculation he relates a story about a guy up in the Midlands who is doing very nicely thank you by copying jazz records and flogging them to modern jazz fanatics.
    Kenny by this time was drumming aboard the QE1 the New York/Southampton 'ferry' bringing back priceless jazz albums unavailable in the UK. He suggested why didn't I get a recording outfit and go into business. We being avid modern jazz fans from Stan Kenton to Gerry Mulligan etc. were aware that no British record conglomerates could be bothered with jazz, especially modern jazz. It sounded like a lifeline to me and exciting to boot. Can you copy a record? If so, how?

With this in mind I spoke to my dad about acquiring some recording gear. I had little knowledge of what I was suggesting and he had even less. However, times were desperate and I think he saw it as a vague opportunity. Clutching at straws would probably be more descriptive.

Dad was down to his last few hundred pounds and after scouring the phone books we went to the *MSS Recording Company* in Colnbrook, near Heathrow. Sheer luck, we could not have discovered a better company. Dad spent over £600 on equipment that, despite a lengthy demonstration by a charming Mr. Pemberton, I retained only the haziest idea of the four hours tuition. However, I did *now* know the difference between a tape record and a disc cutting machine.

For the aficionados; *that money bought a 2 speed MSS tape deck recorder (Heavy, grey and bombproof), a 12" turntable 78 rpm disc cutter (also bombproof), 3 Reslo ribbon microphones with stands. Two drums of cables, ten cutting styli and an assortment of blank acetate discs, various sizes.*

£600 in 1951 was a lot of dosh, had I wasted dad's money? In retrospect and considering his inability to comprehend the mysterious equipment he had paid for, his faith in me was astounding. But dad was no stick in the mud. He could foresee the possibilities of recording amateur singers and groups of which there was an abundance to be found in and around the London area. Being able to make a record for them was a prospect that actually excited him. Also, we would be the only outlet for people seeking that service. Given different times, dad could have been a theatre impresario. He proved to have the ability to listen and advise amateur talent with enthusiasm. Something I lacked. Given a pint, or two, he could put over a song or two at a family party, especially at Christmas-time. Of course, the bootlegging side of the equation remained a mystery to him.

After much experimentation, I discovered I had a knack for the mysterious art of acetate disc cutting and even more so, an ear for sound mixing. In less than a year, the backroom of our house on the Bypass in the London borough of East Ham was a mass of wires and machinery. Two Vortexion tape decks were added to the gear.

The business was really thriving, we up-graded to a professional acetate disc cutting lathe. This was a huge console that dad picked up at MSS. It was in a bare bones condition, albeit brand new. I now had 3-speed cutting capability.

For the aficionados;
I can do no better than Wikipedia to explain an acetate disc;

Unlike ordinary vinyl records, which are quickly formed from lumps of plastic by a mass-production moulding process, a so-called acetate disc is created by using a recording lathe to cut an audio-signal-modulated groove into the surface of a special lacquer-coated blank disc, a real-time operation requiring expensive, delicate equipment and expert skill for good results. They are made for special purposes, almost never for sale to the general public. They can be played on any normal record player but will suffer from wear more quickly than vinyl. Some acetates are highly prized for their rarity, especially when they contain unpublished material.

I hope Mr. Wikipedia doesn't mind my quoting this; I could never have done it so succinctly. I like the bit about 'expert skill' – I could have included that on my CV.

Recording onto 45rpm or 78rpm formats from a tape recorder is a known quantity – around 3 minutes. At long play, the amount of grooves on a 12" blank can be varied to fit the material being recorded. However, if these grooves are set too close, excessive sound level from the source material could cause the cut groove to vary in amplitude, even infiltrate into the adjacent groove, result; playback needle will jump - disc ruined. If the grooves are kept perpetually wide the quantity of material being transferred would be much less. At the same time, the farther away the grooves can be kept from the middle of the disc the better. Less land to cover increases hiss level.

Thus varigroove is required and it must be dominated by the source material level. In simple terms; for the quiet bits the grooves can be closer. For loud bits, grooves need to be further apart. An additional playback head on the source tape deck can be positioned before the actual playback head feeding the cutting styli. An indication of excessive level can then be fed to the scrolling device on the recorder. The grooves can be widened to accept a higher sound level BEFORE the actual playback head information reaches the cutting stylus. Thus, Happiness is achieved!

However, as previously explained, trying to cram too much time onto a disc the less land it covers resulting in an unacceptable hiss. After hearing a 1950 LP Duke Ellington Orchestra, which was, at that time, the finest quality I had ever heard. *(Masterpieces By Ellington - released Columbia Records 1950 - re-released 2004 Sony-CK 87043.)* I decided to write to Columbia Records in New York outlining my unwanted hiss problem.

I was stunned two months later to receive a package from their technical department advising me to use 'hot cut'. I doubt you would get a response of that ilk today. Technical details and some wire samples were included were enclosed. It involved wrapping DC heated ultra-thin SWG wire around the cutting styli enabling the needle to cut through the acetate like a hot knife through butter. A method of collecting the swarf was also fitted using a miniature vacuum cleaner. Before, if often rounded back to clog the styli - another blank ruined. I suppose it's too late to offer my sincere thanks to the department that helped me. I should have done so at the time.

However, fitting these innovations was beyond my capabilities. At one point the instruction sheet got mislaid - was it seven turns of SWG grade 10, or ten turns of SWG grade 7? I had a dear friend, Don Worman, and we spent many candle burning hours; involving many cutting styli shrivelled with too much heat, not to mention probably sixty, or so, ruined blank acetates.

During these lengthy sessions, Don taught me the art of admiring the poor relation of the song writing business, the lyricist. Don recounted to me the famed story of the first night of SHOWBOAT (1927) in New York, when a lady went up to Jerome Kern's wife and said;

'I loved your husband's song Ol Man River'

To which Oscar Hammerstein's wife retorted;

'No my husband wrote Ol Man River, Jerome wrote (she sang) dah dah dah-dah . . . .'

My regard for the lyricist has never diminished. Alan J. Lerner is surely among the all-time top three with hits like My Fair Lady. Gigi. On a Clear Day. Camelot etc. In his biography, there is a terrific story concerning his dad who was a very rich and successful Wall Street banker. Unfortunately, he had a terrible health record and when asked to sign to agree to a forty seventh operation he did so and said . . . *'When it gets to fifty – sell'*.

With my new set-up intact, I was recording groups, singers and amateur shows on a regular basis (with a bit of Kenny Clare inspired bootlegging on the side). Dad was the business brain; I was the boffin in the backroom, from which my sisters were strictly banned, although Cindy recollects (at the age of ten) watching the swarf swirling into the vacuum tube as a record was being cut. She had been instructed to 'sit down, shut up and above all, don't touch anything'. Even to this day she recollects my harsh tone of voice. She also remembers my finally giving in, allowing her to make a record of 'I Saw Mummy Kissing Santa Klaus' for her mummy. So, I wasn't such an ogre, after all?

Kenny Clare was now playing with Johnny Dankworth. He asked me to record one of their radio broadcasts, which I did. Some days later, both Johnny and Cleo Laine would trek out to East Ham, where mum would make them a cup of tea while they listened to a playback of their broadcast on one of my tape machines.

    Today's iPod generation would be astounded to learn that there were only a handful of tape recorders around in those days. The BBC probably didn't even record live broadcasts and presumably not in the business of starting a trend in that direction.

I was later to work with Cleo on her Special at ATV, a super one hour programme exploiting her talents and direct by Colin Clewes. I also was sound director on her Muppet Show. I recounted the East Ham Bypass story, I think it rang a distant bell? However, even more recently(2017) my daughter worked at Cleo's workshop theatre at *The Stables, Wavendon* and yes, she did remember the East Ham visits with some nostalgia.

One unforgettable gig was to record an end-of-term Sub-Lieutenants show at the Royal Naval College in Greenwich. There were forty or fifty subs of both sexes in the show called *Alpine Holiday* was cleverly written by Ronnie Baker and Don Styles with a heavy nautical vein. Lots of sub-lieutenants jokes were craftily included. Don Styles was actually my friend Don Worman as previously mentioned. In real life Don was an assessor for the 600 Group. If you flew him over the Firth of Forth Bridge, he'd access its value to the nearest fifty quid.

The standard of performance at the Royal Naval College shows was quite high. The theatre in the lush grounds of the college was very posh. For a whole day, I recorded (on seven and half ips Vortexion) all the musical items using close microphone technique. Then 'on the night' with the audience present, I put three foot microphones at the front of the stage for the entire performance not forgetting a slung microphone for audience reaction.

For show, dad helped me rig our entire recording kit two Vortexion tape recorders and a portable disc cutter, (which wasn't used).

Later that week I edited the previously recorded close up singing items into the evening performance. Finding it now necessary to edit the entire show down to fifty minutes allowing it to be transferred to a 12" acetate.

Here's one I made earlier!

To my astonishment we had orders from the cast and audience for over 140 LP's. I think this quantity was due to dad telling the Subs that he would post the LP 'COD' to their home address so that their parents would pay (brilliant move dad). Before this order was completed, the next sub-show was ready to record. In all, five sub-show tapes filled the back room and I was often cutting well into the early hours.

After continually cutting the same disc over and over, it is little wonder that now, many years later, I still have those songs and lyrics swirling around in my head. Modern jazz addict Alan Shillum (later my brother-in-law) designed beautiful sleeves for the albums, in return for jazz records. Dad even had boxes made out of plywood for transportation by post to the sub-lieutenant's home addresses.

Incidentally, Alan Shillum, after an exciting career as a jobbing journalist rose to the heady heights of Managing Editor of the Daily Mirror. The tales he could tell about Robert Maxwell….but he keeps shtum. He was (and still is) a very good artist. He has probably the finest collection of Modern Jazz in Europe. Some albums are worth hundreds. The shelving in his office is so strong it actually *is* bomb-proof.

Although the recording business was thriving, I still found time for the odd bit of boot legging. I never considered it to be illegal or offensive. In my mind I was even providing a public service. Modern Jazz albums were totally unavailable in the UK. I had a customer base of 5-600 modern jazz fans. I remember Christmas 1952, our front room was swamped with over 500 Christmas cards. The modern jazz blurb sheets I sent out would contain truthful warts-and-all reviews of the albums available.

Later I began to accept six 78-rpm records (good condition only) in exchange for one acetate jazz album. I amassed many hundreds of 78's and opened a small record shop to dispose of them. The shop in Romford Road, Manor Park (east London) also became the disc cutting centre. All the equipment from mum and dad's house in East Ham was transferred to the shop's back room. It was here that my experimentations with hot-cut formulated.

All night cutting sessions were the norm and many friends (including the aforementioned Dennis Sullivan and Al Shillum) would congregate there to yap and listen, even occasionally to buy. Drink or drugs were NEVER involved just music, music, music.

The profit ratio connected with the 78 rpm record exchanges was quite poor, especially, after postage and the inevitable breakages, but the enterprise generated many friends and brought many fans together.

I advertised my recording services regularly in The Musical Express. My ads were always 'unusual' i.e. *'is that a flying saucer? No – it's another Ted Scott disc being expressly delivered . . . etc'*. Silly, but it brought in business.

Advertising Manager Percy Dickens foresaw the advent of commercial television years before it came and wanted to set me up in a Soho studio recording jingles and suchlike. Regretfully I never went down that road. Who knows what I could have become . . . but then again, look what I did become!

Because it was necessary to scroll a gap between tracks on a 12" record, it was imperative that constant hands-on attention must be paid. At the end of track one, scroll an eighth of an inch before the next track begins. Considering that perhaps fifty records would be made of the same material it was obvious that those songs became embedded in your head. Years later, I can hum all the Sub-Lieutenant Shows. Add my years of working on television music shows where with recording, post mixing and eventual sound dubbing songs and light entertainment shows there are masses of this stuff often reverberating around my head.

With the record shop now well established the bootleg side of the business was (ahem) curtailed after a not very friendly visit by a representative of Esquire Records who had just started releasing some modern jazz stuff in 1958.

The shop remained open but the shelves no longer offered bootleg stuff. The amateur recording stuff was beginning to bore me slightly. They were usually well below par. Dad was terrific with amateurs; as I said earlier, he would have made a great impresario. Sometimes, during a playback of something recorded the night before he would request hearing it just one more time. I had to leave the room whilst dad extolled the virtues of the performer(s) even offering tips on vocal improvement, often with surprising results.

Around that time I was doing a regular acetate cutting service for Radio Luxembourg. Pre-released 45rpm acetates were sent to me where I would cut several copies to be distributed to the Luxembourg in-house DJs. Many of which never reached the airwaves.

Learning that Radio Luxembourg had a vacancy for a sound assistant. I decided to take the bull by horns and join the professional world. And yes, dad set up the interview for me again and for the last time. Mum and dad still had the record shop to play with and, stupidly, I allowed all the equipment to be sold off. Today that antiquated disc cutting console would be welcome in a museum or I would still have something to play with.

IN RETROSPECT;
If I were to dedicate my ramblings to anybody it could well be my dad who had faith in my vague venture into disc cutting. But we both would have preferred giving it to my friend Kenny Clare. Without his casual advice I could well be still burring spark plugs in some remote garage somewhere.

***

4. Radio Luxembourg – the station of the stars.

BASED IN MID-EUROPE, Radio Luxembourg beamed English speaking transmissions from 6pm until the early hours. At that time, commercial radio was verboten in the UK. The BBC was stuck in the 'Home Service' and 'Third Programme' mode. Radio Luxembourg filled the gap.

With the advent of rock and roll, the record programmes were eagerly listened to. Reception could sometimes be almost un-intelligible or more often as clear as a bell. The great majority of transmissions were sponsored record programmes. Eagerly awaited by pop music fans, the Top Twenty was broadcast every Sunday night live from Luxembourg itself, virtually the only genuine chart up-date.

The remainder of the English broadcast material emanated from the studios in Hertford Street, in the heart of the Mayfair district. Of the twenty or thirty staff, none of us had ever been to Luxembourg.

The racing driver Stirling Moss had a town house in the mews at the rear of the Luxembourg studios. This was where we parked without restriction, no meters, no wardens hiding behind lamp posts . . . ah! Happy days. One of the girls in accounts occasionally emulated a racing driver. I recollect Stirling washing his car down before staring in amazement as Mia zoomed out of the narrow mews with many cars parked at 40 mph . . . **in reverse!**

Once, Mia offered me a lift to Green Park Station. The traffic in Piccadilly was tailed back and in her impatience, she tapped the rear end of a police car . . . twice!! The driver got out and after a cursory chat, politely waved her to go ahead of him. Mia could charm as well as drive crazily.

38 Hertford Street contained two studios; four edit suites and four floors of office space. On the lower ground floor were several edit suites. These were four times larger than a telephone kiosk, no windows and walls covered in sound proofing material. Producers likened them to Japanese prisoner of war camp solitary confinement boxes.

At the end of the corridor was what seemed like, a large cupboard. An aged gentleman named Fred appeared to never leave this location. Fred provided tea and buns at, seemingly, every hour of the long working day. He was also an active bookies runner. I don't think managing director Clement Cave, or office manager Reggie Belcher ever gave Fred much business, so that only left our executive producer Geoffrey Everett in the frame (as it were).

Also, on this level was the sound store and office. A capacious cupboard herein served as an echo chamber. Selected sound from either of the two studios would be fed into a loudspeaker at one end of this cupboard to be picked up by a microphone at the other. Crude, but effective. It was difficult to make a telephone call from the sound office when a studio was in use, with Cliff Richard echoing around or Pete Murray in Studio B wanted a ghost effect for his record programme could prove challenging.

I started work at Radio Luxembourg in 1955 on seven pounds fifteen shillings a week, leaving in December 1959 as head of sound (grandly labelled *Chief Engineer)* on £20 per week. The word overtime didn't exist in 38 Hertford

Street, although, later I managed to persuade Geoffrey Everett to pay five shillings an hour past 48 worked hours.

You didn't work in the media then for money, it was hard graft and worth a fortune in experience. We recorded DJ programmes all the week then drove all over the country recording various quiz shows during weekends. Never less than sixty hours a week, often considerably more. But, boy, was it great fun!

A typical day was Jack Jackson, say, three programmes in the morning, Pete Murray in the afternoon and Alan Freeman or Sam Costa after him. Normally three one hour programmes were recorded in roughly that period with added time for tape changes.

Re-takes were minimal and rehearsals non-existent. The record company guys would 'direct'. S. A. Beecher-Stevens did it for EMI while Frank Barnes represented Decca. He would arrive with his PA and a stack of records, or occasionally freshly cut blanks. We NEVER played a record all through. Each disc had a pre-arranged chinagraph mark for in and out cues, usually about thirty seconds of the record's best part, then onto to the next plug.

Colin Eldred and I were the spinners. With headphones you would place the styli on the first chinagraph mark, find the 'in' cue and hold the disc (which was on a felt mat) as the turntable turned. The other hand was on your fader. As the previous record ended, the dee jay would spiel from hastily written notes or ad lib. The intro to the next disc was usually obvious, Frank Barnes would wave an arm and you released the disc and faded up. Before the second chinagraph point loomed up, you were cueing up the next disc. Then Frank would wave for you to fade down, he then cued the dee jay with the other hand. Frank Barnes thoroughly enjoyed this task, it got him out of the office to play producer.

Later, I became the sound mixer on these sessions. This involved fading the dee jay up and down and performing the edit ritual if a fluff happened.

For the aficionados, the edit process was as follows;
Rewind the tape to ten seconds before the required edit. Hold the tape off the recording head with a pencil. Play tape to the edit point, cue the DJ and quickly release the pencil to allow the tape to bounce onto the recording head to start recording a millisecond before the previous fluff which is now erased.

This operation was a knack – ten 'A' levels couldn't help. Talking of fluff, Alan Freeman's nick-name actually derived at Radio Luxembourg. Alan had a terrific radio voice and was a really nice guy but he sure earned that nick-name.

In the odd hours at Hertford Street when the studios were not in use for record shows, we would start to compile and edit the outside broadcast material. On the Ted Heath band show for instance; a selection of quarter inch tapes recorded at Wandsworth Town Hall were cut and 'pasted' (to use a modern term) with pre-recorded announcements and the Gillette commercial blurb at the front, middle and end.

Despite losing time for spooling sixteen inch reels, a fifteen minute show took around thirty minutes to compile in this fashion, totally ready for transmission. The speed was due to one's ability to edit quarter inch tape. Having quickly assessed the edit point, a chinagraph dot was placed on both sides of the edit. The joining tape was cut diagonally into roughly an inch in length before placing over the edit point, also cut diagonally.

An editing block could be used for this function but we preferred to hold the two pieces of tape in one hand, both dots synchronised, then use the other hand to cut with a one sided razor blade. Sounds complicated but wasn't. This rarely took longer than five seconds. Pity we weren't timed like Formula One teams for wheel changes; we could have probably got it down to four seconds!

All material recorded at Hertford Street was flown to Luxembourg on 16 inch reels of tape, recorded at 30 inches per second. The quantity of tapes in transit was an enormous air freight commitment. The used tapes came back by boat and land. The tapes were constantly re-cycled. Thus, a one hour tape ready for re-use after block erasure, could contain as many is sixty manual edits.

Sometimes a producer would edit a tape after it left our hands. If that edit had not been done well (never happened with us sound guys!), the join would 'bump' over the heads affecting the new sound and necessitating a re-take. To obviate the same thing happening at the same point, the tape could be pushed into the head with a pencil just as the join went through. We got good value from our pencils!

Brand new reels of tape were strictly rationed looked and looked upon enviously. An old reel of tape had to be pretty well condemned before replacement.

Some months after I joined the sound staff and after much pressure from the Musicians Union, Radio Luxembourg had their needle time cut. This caused a massive gap in the scheduling and compelled the management to seek alternative programme material. Thus, many music and quiz shows were hastily devised and recorded for later transmission.

Over the following years we were recording just about every band and singer in the land. Some of these were in the studios but mostly on outside recordings throughout the country. You could be in Birmingham on the Friday morning. Rig, test and rehearse in the afternoon recording one or more shows at night. Next day, it would be Manchester, same schedule. Sundays were usually audience related shows, Hughie Green; People are Funny; Max Wall's Laughter in Court, Singalong with Izzy Bonn etc. Back to

London late Sunday night, park the vehicle and turn up next morning for Jack Jackson or Sam Costa, whatever. You perceive how that cheap overtime rate was well devised by the management?

For the aficionados;
A breakdown of the recording gear used for outside work. The van was similar in size to the modern day smaller 'white van' – except it was emblazoned with the RADIO LUXEMBOURG motif, attracting lots of car hooting on the major roads of Great Britain.
We were a two man crew alternating driving and resting. The gear consisted of a twelve channel rotary fader mixing console. Two heavy duty loudspeaker monitors. Two (bomb-proof) EMI TR90 tape recorders, a cacophony of microphones with coils of cable, reels of recording tapes and coils of rope. Why rope? To assist slinging microphones for audience reaction in various church halls, working men's clubs, town halls and assembly rooms.
We did not supply a public address system. This task was usually farmed out to local contractors or, in the case of bigger venues (Wandsworth, Luton, Poplar and other town halls) they had their own PA equipment. Lastly, a good supply of blankets for those lengthy drives back to London for the resting half of the team.
In the early hours after a recording we had to dash back to London. I was driving and Sam Cartmer (then head of sound) was asleep in the passenger seat (we didn't have seat belts in those days). I must have dozed momentarily and drove straight over a small humped roundabout. We lurched crazily. Sam, flung against the windscreen woke up (to put it mildly). He asked what happened (an abbreviated description!), 'Sorry, Sam – had to avoid a fox' He looked at the very disturbed gear in the back of the van . . . 'Some fox' he muttered.

The management always booked us into good 4 and 5 star hotels, I had never stayed in a posh hotel before. First time (I think, Manchester) I went down to breakfast alone and the waiter asked me if I was a guest. A guest?

Confused, I said no and was charged for breakfast, best part of two days' pay.

We traversed the country every weekend from Southampton to Edinburgh come rain or shine and even snowdrifts, once it took thirteen hours getting back from Newcastle to Hertford Street for a DJ session. And we loved every minute of it. Some of the programmes and band shows that come to mind.

 Ted Heath Orchestra
 Ronnie Aldrich and the Squadronaires
 Ken Mackintosh Orchestra.
 Lyons Mint Chocs Show.
 The David Whitfield Show.
 Norrie Paramour Strings.
 Big Ben Banjo Band
 Billy's Banjo Band.
 Primo Scala's Accordion Band
 Cliff Richard & the Shadows
 Kenny Ball's Jazzmen.
 Chris Barber with Ottilie Patterson.
 Humphrey Lyttleton Jazz Band.
 Joe Loss and his Orchestra.
 Harry Gold's Pieces of Eight.
 The Eddie Calvert Shows
 Frankie Vaughan Shows
 Anne Shelton series.
 Ruby Murray series.
 (I bet I've missed out someone?)

This list constitutes a gigantic number of musical items – many of which still whirl around my head at odd times.

For the aficionados;
How do you record a big band the size and complexity of Ted Heath with just twelve channels allowing no more than twelve microphones? This was our plot;
 Bass, piano, guitar and piano - one mic each.
 Four trumpets - one mic. Half-moon the trumpets.

Four trombones - one mic. Half-moon the trombones.
Drums . . . three mics.
One bass drum, one hi-hat and one overall.
Vocal and announcer . . . one mic.
Saxophones . . . one mic. Five Saxes sat in a circle with an omni-directional microphone in the middle. When a saxophone had a solo, he would stand and lean in. Otherwise they were self-balancing. That still left one fader for unforeseens. If no unforeseens, use that extra mic placed above the saxophone microphone for solo work.

Of course, none of these could be grouped as with later television rigs, so it was imperative to get the mix right. It was going onto quarter inch, once recorded no going back. Years later this would have been a frightening prospect. Being a stickler for a good drum sound, I recollect at ATV on a big music programme using ten microphones on the drum kit alone. The exception was Buddy Rich. He pooh poohed multi-microphone rigs. He virtually sound mixed his own drum sound. On the Buddy Rich Muppet Show where he had a drum duel with Animal, just one boom over Buddy's kit and one boom over Ronnie Verrell's kit was used. Ronnie being out of vision of course but eagerly watched by Frank Oz who was working Animal.

Humphrey Lyttleton called me the 'butcher of Hertford Street' His 45 minute show would consist of five or six items. Trouble was, most of Humph's repertoire was often twenty five minutes in length. i.e. 16 bars intro. 16 bars clarinet, 16 bars trumpet, 16 bars piano, 16 more bars clarinet and a few extra choruses ad lib if they felt like it.
I don't think I ever let a bad edit through that an audience would perceive. But I can quite understand a musician hearing a playback and thinking; *'What the hell happened to my middle 16 bars – my best bit?'*

ANNE SHELTON was a war-time forces favourite (along with Vera Lynn), Anne was a regular visitor to Radio

Luxembourg. Accompanied by the Geoff Love orchestra, she delighted us all with her lovely sense of humour and her terrific voice. Her sister Jo could have been a great singer as well, but I believe she suffered from shyness?

Anne, like many of her contemporaries sang a huge repertoire of songs without the need for re-takes or tracking. An affliction which touches many modern days stars. Laying down a voice track on multi-track tape recorders sometimes line by line then mixing between them for a few hours to get the best version of each segment is now a common occurrence. I would have a problem to remember any occasion where Anne Shelton asked for a re-take. But in all fairness, why would an artiste not take advantage of modern day technology to attain a perfect outcome. With world sales of albums reaching into the many millions, the financial incentive is huge.

In the slack off-peak advertising periods, we made filler programmes, Interviews with Frank Sinatra, Johnny Ray, Mel Torme and Stan Kenton. Geoffrey Everett, let me compile whole programmes, giving me the opportunity to act 'producer' and make up several 1-hour shows using these interviews interspersed with record tracks.

Yes, I actually met Stan Kenton! I had a signed photo that he had sent me in the forties. I showed it to him and he told me he actually remembered signing it, adding, he didn't have too many European fans in those days (Stan could be an old smoothie!). He could also talk nine to the dozen.

Later, I interspersed his dialogue with Kenton tracks to make up (I think) three one hour programmes. Geoffrey Everett allowed me to edit three one hour programmes by myself. This was a labour of sheer love. If Stan mentioned June Christy, I'd start a Christy track under dialogue so her vocal started as he finished yapping. Often, he'd back reference something and I'd have to start all over again. No overtime payments were permitted for those sessions!

Frank Sinatra wasn't particularly verbose and only the charm of David Jacobs got an interview barely worth broadcasting. Possibly, Mr Sinatra wasn't too keen to discuss his personal habits, which I think was the crux of David's tack. He arrived with only one minder, an aged agent of some sort. Years later he would be accompanied by an entourage and you would be unable to get near him. I do remember casually admiring his sports jacket – was it Cecil Gee's? He nearly replied, but didn't.

Johnny Ray was big at that time. His recording of 'CRY' sold millions. He seemed quite a nice guy albeit (it seemed to me) tone deaf. Hearing his 'life story' the crying was understandable.

Still one of the most underrated singers of the age was Mel Torme known as 'The Velvet Fog'. When he came to Hertford Street to be interviewed, Pat, our gorgeous blonde but sometimes hazy receptionist, put him in the waiting room and forgot about him.

Pat always wore a billowing short skirt and the guys down in the edit basement offered called up to her to ostensibly ask something. She would come out of her little reception booth and stand at the top of the stairs allowing the guys downstairs to look up her skirt. I doubt she ever realized.

Anyway, she put Mel in the waiting room. Half an hour later, wondering if he was a no-show, we finally discovered him in the gloomy room where apparently he had been engrossed in *Country Life.* Mr. Torme was a really nice guy, still one of my top three male vocalists.

All of these live musical shows that had to fill the needle time space were in addition to the normal Luxembourg DJ shows with Peter Murray, Jack Jackson, Alan Freeman, Sam Costa, Beryl Reid, Dickie Murdoch, Charles (Bud) Tingwell, from Emergency Ward Ten, Eric Winstone's Butlins kid's shows, Godfrey Winn's classical hour and many more.

Even Freddie Mills, the famous boxer had a record show. Freddie, never without a smile, once left the building to discover a traffic jam outside. The road opposite (Down Street) was grid-locked with Hertford Street owing to a broken down van. Taxis and cars were hooting and shouting at each other. Freddie, with his instantly recognizable square jaw, stepped into the road and got drivers to reverse, pull forward an inch, *'you – stay where you are'* etc. You didn't argue with Freddie Mills. I don't remember Freddie ever needing a re-take. He was once world light heavyweight champion and died tragically (and certainly mysteriously) at the age of 46.

Beryl Reid had a rough script but rarely kept to it. Her rogue-ish laugh came across at home as if she were sitting next to you. Sometimes, visitors would be doing a studio tour. If Beryl was in mid-announcement she would often ad-lib a request for say, a honeymoon couple and spice her dialogue with several rather juicy words or situations. The shocked visitors would leave in haste. We'd edit out the naughty bits later.

Pete Murray was a terrifically handsome, debonair guy, massively successful as a dee jay, although not many people know he won the top acting award at the BBC for his portrayal as a scarred Battle of Britain Spitfire pilot. Pete could have made a big-time actor but was typecast in the dee jay mould. A situation he was most unhappy with. I often came across both Beryl and Pete many years later when I was working on *Celebrity Squares* at ATV.

Jack Jackson (allegedly not renowned for 'standing his corner') invited Sam Cartmer and myself to his farm in Hertfordshire where we saw a different Jack Jackson. He had built a studio and wanted us to approve it. We had dinner with his family, a resplendent affair equal to a five star hotel. His children kissed him and their mother on arrival at the table. We left with a present and payment for our 'advice'. Oh yes, a different Jack Jackson to the one at the studio.

These DJ's at Radio Luxembourg were the only source for people to hear the latest pops. They were the original song pluggers. Today, with global communication it is difficult to comprehend a period when record sales and plugging were in the hands of individual human beings.

Guys like Alan Davison of EMI records had their fingers firmly on the pulse. They knew everything that was released as they bombarded the record outlets with their wares. Their opinions were listened to and trusted. If they said 'such-and-such' would make the charts, but probably only halfway up, the stores would order accordingly. It was the personal touch, something sadly missing today. Alan did ten years at EMI, which he described as his most important years before starting up 'Lightning Records'.

Radio Luxembourg had a one hour listener's request programme every evening and people were invited to write in with a request. Often none arrived - one of the reasons being people addressed their letter to Radio Luxembourg c/o BBC London. The BBC used to save this mail until a sack was full then return it to the GPO with a note *'Not known at this address'.*

Thus it was apparent that someone at the beeb had a sense of humour! It's probably not hot news by now but sackfuls of these request items were later 'sold' to the cheaper football pool companies.

Horace Bachelor was also a famous Luxembourg name. His *'Infra-draw'* method promised football pool success. Producer George Harman and I were convinced there must be something in his method as he regularly won dividends himself every week. We finally plucked up the courage to ask him whether our close association merited a special bit of inside information. He listened to our woes carefully and said; *'Just send five shilling to Horace Bachelor . . .'* etc.

Actually, his winning lines were always on cheaper pools (farthing a line or even eight lines a penny) and often his permutation investments exceeded his winnings. But, he could always say, truthfully, 'last week I won two first dividends and six second dividends'

Horace did his own voice over adverts. Vivian Winstanley Gale, our very posh sound technician once gave Horace the name of his (Harley Street) dentist as Horace's dentures emitted a whistle on certain words. Horace thanked him for his concern before boarding his waiting chauffeured Rolls Royce. He probably figured that distinctive whistle got him better listening figures.

Vivian came to us with burning enthusiasm to be 'in sound'. He had served as an intelligence officer during the war (a Lt-Colonel, I think?) so despite being 'of an age' we took him on. Although not musically inclined, Vivian had a fervent desire to sound mix.

During a rehearsal and set-up period of The Ken Mackintosh *'Lyon's Mint Choc Show'* in some northern venue (The Winter Gardens?) I let Vivian have a go at the console during a band rehearsal. Ken came in during this and after looking at me with a wince, turned to Viv to ask him where his saxophones had gone.

Vivian (with faders all over the place) explained to Ken that the auditorium we were in had acoustical problems exacerbated by the glass filled dome roof, he further gave Ken some mathematical theories concerning sound waves. Ken stared at him before asking;

*'Yeah, but where's my ****** saxophones?'*

Ken Mackintosh was a brilliant alto player. The sax section was his love. Get that sounding right and he was as happy as Larry. Ditto for Ted Heath and trombones, Ronnie Aldrich and the rhythm section, it was wise to even accentuate these sections when they popped in for a listen at rehearsals.

Vivian Gale eventually left to become Head of Sound at Granada TV. As HOD he was probably terrific but he shouldn't be let loose on a sound mixing console. I have vague memories of a jazz band emanating from that region where (bravely) no microphones were in shot. It remains in my mind as an appalling mess. Viv was a perfect gentleman. I took him out on an OB somewhere in Newcastle. On the arduous journey he sat in the passenger seat holding his walking stick and still wearing a bowler hat. On arrival at the venue I started to unload but Viv found a porter, gave him a ten bob note and got him to do it. Why didn't we think of that years ago?

On the way back to London we stopped at a typical northern fish and chip shop that had a small table for eating in. After a delicious meal Viv asked the chippie proprietor to please convey his compliments to the chef. I really believe it was his first visit to such an establishment.

Vivian spoke perfect French and sometimes liaised with the people in Luxembourg giving top twenty up-dates on the telephone. I recollect one day he asked whether he could have the afternoon off. Being very late notice, I enquired why;

'I'm getting married at Caxton Hall at one o'clock, old bean.'

He was marrying the French girl at the other end of the Luxembourg line. Viv drove back in his fantastic Railton sports car by six pm for a recording session. It was rumoured that Viv's parents owned half of Ebury Street, W1.

The music shows were a Godsend for us sound guys. The chance to sound mix top bands and groups was invaluable experience which paid massive dividends later in life. Where else today would anybody get the opportunity we enjoyed?

The Ted Heath Band shows achieved something of a record. One hundred and fifty-six programmes sponsored by Gillette, ran continuously for three years. We recorded three shows at a time, always in Wandsworth Town Hall between 0930 and 1200. Either Dennis Lotus, Bobby Britton or Lita Roza usually did one song per show. Ted was a charming old thing, although I believe he ran the band like a rod of iron. He frequently sacked Jackie Armstrong, the trombone player, for being late. But, Jackie always showed up next time as if nothing had happened.

After we had set up the gear, Ted would come into our adjoining room and listen to the balance. Ted's hearing, after years of fronting a big band was not good. He would put an ear up against the loudspeaker, turn to us and say *'More trombones'.* We would comply. Then he wanted more saxophones then more trumpets then more rhythm - then . . . more trombones.

When the level was deafening and certainly over modulated, Ted would leave us, seemingly happy. At this point we would revert all the faders to where they were. We always used the small hall (of two) at Wandsworth. Apparently the hire was £2.15 a session, the large hall was nearly double! Geoffrey Everett looked after the pennies!

In Hertford Street, we had a sound crew of six, of which (by 1958) I was the Chief Engineer! This title will be regarded with humour by people who know me. I'd probably burn myself with a soldering iron! Often technical letters came from listeners requesting information concerning reception criteria etc. I often buried these letters in the Request Programme sacks. It is astounding now to think that on several request programmes nobody at Hertford Street could find the sacks of listeners record requests. Sometimes we would make up names and messages. My (fictional) aunt in Gravesend was a constant requester.

However, much to the managements delight, one of the first things I ordained was that henceforth all tapes would be recorded at 15 ips thereby virtually cutting air-freight charges by half. I won my Chief Engineer spurs by saving the company dosh.

Every programme we made had commercial slots. Voice-over artistes were regular visitors. Names that come to mind are, Patrick Allen, the Canadian who starred in many movies. Another Canadian, Gerry Wilmot who lived in a fantastic apartment in Mayfair. Gordon Davies, him of the silky voice and smooth manner. Off-stage Gordon was terrific fun. John Brabham was a well-used voice as was John Benson who later did stacks of television voice-overs. Barry . . .? (Can anybody help?). He was another smoothie voice. He would come into the studio an hour before needed to play on our magnificent Bechstein grand piano in studio A. Often we'd come back from lunch to find Barry in dreamland, cigarette holder in mouth, eyes closed emulating and playing excerpts from Noel Coward.

The husband and wife team of John Witty and Genniene Graham were always around. John, as handsome as any film star, did the Horace Bachelor voice-overs. Although Horace did his own blurb, it always ended with John saying; *'Keynsham, that's K.E.Y.N.S.H.A.M Keynsham, Bristol'* Remember? (Well, I guess you'd have to be of an age!).

Genniene did masses of girlie voice overs. She was an extremely beautiful young lady. Both she and John could easily have been in movies or twenty years down the line starring in television.

We did some memorable musical programmes with the husband and wife team of Teddy Johnson and Pearl Carr. Teddy hosted record shows as well. Pearl often quietly told Teddy to watch his pitch, or other niggling things. But it would be difficult to ruffle his feathers. In any case, they were both obviously very much in love.

Teddy's brother Bryan Johnson won the *Eurovision Song Contest* in the fifties with *'Looking High-High-High'*. Bryan had a programme on Luxembourg where the viewers were asked to complete a limerick of which he would sing the first three lines then say *'That was a cute little rhyme – can you complete the last line?'* Some of the entrants were . . . interesting, but rarely transmittable!

All programmes were assigned a producer. They booked artistes, oversaw scripts, shaped the look of the show to fit in commercials, attended the recording session before checking the final show preceding despatch to Luxembourg, a busy job, to say the least. Today, an office of several people would cover that workload. In almost every case, these producers were ordinary guys and girls from backgrounds that had nothing to do with entertainment.

Some names spring to mind; Adam Leys left early on to write. Joy Sharpen went, I think, to ITV. Of Peter Fox, I know not. George Harmer opened a florist outlet. Peter Pritchett-Brown left to become transmission controller at Southern TV. Tom Masson, one of the rare producers with 'previous' returned to the comfort of the BBC. Tom handled the Winifred Atwell series. One evening after I had completed an edit session he settled down in his checking booth listening to a final playback to ensure the tape was ready for transmission. At some time during his arduous task, Tom having had a jar or two before working (inexplicably) fell asleep.

The office cleaners found him the following morning, still a'slumber. The tape reel was still going round and round but the tape had completely disintegrated and the air in the small checking room contained thousands of small particles of floating tape. Even Tom had an inch layer on his inert body. The EMI recording console (a BTR 1, also bombproof) was red hot, luckily it didn't catch fire.

That show was lost for all time. However, we regurgitated items from other Winifred Atwell Shows and no great harm was done, certainly Winnie never knew. Lew Levensen, her husband-manager rarely allowed Winnie to waste time listening to the radio. They were on the road too much.

We did the first Winifred Atwell Show at the Kursaal Ballroom, Southend. Lew had 'found' a new star and he was to have his first broadcast that night. It was Matt Monroe. I remember Lew telling us about his 'new find';

'He's like that Frank Sinatra geezer, but more relaxed!'

We reckoned that Lew got him a job on the buses for a short time so he could reveal him as 'the singing bus conductor'. After the show, Lew asked Sam Cartmer (still head of sound) who mixed the show, how to get to the railway station. Sam replied;

'I haven't got a clue, Lew, why not ask your ******* bus conductor'?

On another occasion, Lew admonished Sam for making an error. To which Sam replied; *'If I made as many mistakes as your old lady . . . .'* Sam didn't last too long after that and I got to mix the remainder of the series.

Colin Streeton was probably the most successful Luxembourg producer, both at the station and after. Tall, dark and handsome, his persona was a ready smile and charming manner. Later, he was to leave and open his own production company. I remember doing a freelance job for him on a documentary for the Post Office. The secret of Colin's success was his ability to know everybody's job without letting on.

We had close contact with the advertising agencies. Their representatives always accompanied voice-over people, or artistes, being used for their radio or television commercials. Often no less than two or three suits trying to outdo each other. A *Birds Eye* pea commercial gave us many a chuckle.

They had organized an actor to come in, stand in front of a microphone and putting a finger in their cheek, make a 'popping' noise. This was to accompany the *Birds Eye peas go POP* jingle for a television commercial. We did numerous takes and the three suits, with accompanying posh accents pondered which *pop* carried the most weight. After some fifteen minutes of deliberation they retired to the pub. I'm not sure but I think we edited the wrong one into their copy.

Re-takes were par for the course. But one day I got a lonely executive in to supervise a *Ben Truman Pale Ale* jingle. A four piece quartet, probably Geoff Love, Bert Weedon, Joe Muddel with Jock Cummings on drums. The vocal group was the Bill Brown singers – four of. We had a few rehearsals for balance etc. The executive asked if we could go for one. I put the red light on, ran tape and cued the guys.

It ended something like; *'Ben, Ben, Ben, Ben Truman's Pale Ale, for there are more hops in Ben Truman . . . . .'*

It was a thirty second jingle. I stopped tape, looked at the executive expecting him to find a fault and request a re-take. He pondered, looked at me said; *'Well, I think that was good. Thank you very much'.*

Wait a minute, was he serious? No re-takes. I panicked, what if we lost the tape or accidentally erased it? (That HAD happened). But no, he was adamant. My shock and surprise was only exceeded by the boys in the studio. After he left, I hastily made two safety copies.

Oddly, that jingle accompanied a television advert of a cartoon depicting a London bus with *Ben Truman Pale Ale* painted on the side bumping along. It was transmitted literally hundreds of times over many months. I would have liked to added *'that was take one'* after every transmission.

There was a quietly spoken copywriter with (I think) J. Water Thompson named Kit something-or-the-other. Unlike most advertising bods, Kit wore hippy gear. His claim to fame was 'inventing' the slogan . . . *BEER IS BEST.* Think about it . . . pretty cool for a slogan, short and simple.

One advertising guy, different from all the others was Berny Stringle. A young, handsome, sharply dressed, north London boy with no side, no posh accent and laden to the gunwale's with confidence. He was a breath of fresh air. Berny was to later form his own company and do his own commercials. Among many, the monkey's tea commercials (PG Tips), which he devised, wrote and directed. They were an enormous hit.

Unlike our compatriots at the BBC all this gave us a good insight into the world of advertising preparing us for the future of Independent Television.

Before moving on, I recall a task on my first week at Radio Luxembourg. The BBC had a successful daily cops and robbers drama series *(Dick Barton, Special Agent)* and Luxembourg decided to emulate this by way of a five day a week, quarter hour drama named *John Dark (presumably also a special agent?).* He and two compatriots (similar to Dick Barton) solved various crimes on a daily basis. Our guys worked around two microphones with scripts in hand.

My job was a studio floor effects person. A doorbell, or door opening and closing, knocking on etc etc and other trivial sound effects.

I had access to a script and could amass my effects before we started recording. If there was a fight sequence, an actor could do the effect themselves '*Take that you swine – biff, biff'.* etc. But one sequence called for a body to hit the ground . . . . That was where I came in. I fell on my knees close to an adjacent microphone. Boy, did it hurt. Neil Tucson the very experienced radio producer stopped he recording and kindly showed me how to do a fall. Well you live and learn. Didn't expect that. Wasn't mentioned at the interview.

My friend, Bill Nuttall, the senior ATV sound director also started in similar fashion. Bill was a sound trainee at BBC sound radio and was floor effect person on *The Goon Show (*much more up-market Bill). He also met his future wife Dorothy, who was a BBC sound assistant. A rarity in those days.

The star of *John Dark* was Richard Bebb – one day I discovered he was in a play at ATV and tracked him down to the bar one lunchtime. I crept up behind him and whispered *John Dark, Special Agent.* Boy, was he surprised. He asked me whether my knees ever got better. What a memory.

With today's health and safety rules and regulations, it is doubtful anybody will ever be called upon to re-live my painful experience, but you never know. Media throws up a lot of surprises.

Poor old Roger Wilkinson, operating a fish-pole and up to his chest in a rising tide and implored to 'be sure to protect the microphone, Roger' . . . and he did. But then, I would have done so too.

***

5. Russia interferes.

SINCE ITS INCEPTION, Radio Luxembourg had always tried to be non-political although that was disregarded in the war when Germany used the powerful transmitter to broadcast propaganda to Britain. 'Lord Haw-Haw' conveyed this with a 'posh' British accent. The actual microphone (a huge German Neumann) used by him was on display in the board room at Hertford Street.

In 1957, a high pitched whistle inexplicably blocked English transmissions for three weeks. Financially this nearly crippled the London arm of the station. Advertisers were getting edgy. It was discovered that the whistle was transmitted from Eastern Europe and that the Russians were responsible. It appeared that they had taken umbrage to a comment in a classical music programme hosted by Godfrey Winn.

A brilliant wartime broadcaster, Godfrey lost the tips of several fingers on a convoy to Murmansk during the Second World War. Apparently, on hearing a massive explosion in the middle of the night, he dashed up on deck to see a tanker on fire having been torpedoed. Regretfully, he forgot to don gloves and touched the freezing cold handrails of the ship.

Sometimes, while commenting on classical performers, he often made derogatory remarks about the Soviet Regime. I recollect mixing one of these programmes when he made a disparaging remark about the Soviet's attitude to Moura Lympany, an English concert pianist.

Only after considerable high-level communications with the Russian Embassy did the blocking finally stop, although I believe they were adamant that 'it wasn't us, guv! We were very political correct from then onwards, apart from a DJ show with a young, cheekie chap named Gus Goodwin who had achieved fame on a television music quiz show. The programme was sponsored by a tobacco company and Gus, during his spiel, had made a reference to cancer sticks. Jack Harris, the producer, didn't pick the remark up; he was probably dreaming of the honeymoon he was soon to embark on. I prodded Jack saying *'Can he say cancer sticks Jack*?' Jack, an extremely calm soft-spoken person, went absolutely berserk, dashing into the studio mid-announcement, shouting abuse to a very astonished Gus Goodwin.

Jack Harris was of slight build, balding and probably ex-BBC. When he first appeared with his new girlfriend we were all astounded. She was an absolutely stunning Swedish beauty. We looked at Jack in a new light from then.

My first experience of an enthusiastic audience was recording the radio pilot for the Frankie Vaughan show at Wandsworth Town Hall in the mid to late fifties. Usually our audiences were gathered from clubs, groups or even OAP's, but this show was packed with youngsters and the screams emanating from them were genuine and surprising. Frank Sinatra . . . eat your heart out!

Many years later, in the early eighties at ATV, Frankie Vaughan returned to top the bill on a light entertainment show. The young director (Geoff Sax, now a famed film director) changed the running order on the edit so that Frankie's act was in the middle. He saved the finale of the show for a magician type of act from the *Crazy Horse,* a Paris night club. His speciality was untangling a deckchair – (very funny but mute).

When the head of Light Entertainment (Jon Scoffield) found out, Geoff was compelled to reinstate Frankie, and rightly so. Frankie Vaughan still had it, and the audience (now not so young) let him know too.

Speaking of audiences, The FYFFE'S Banana radio show was innovative insomuch that bananas were thrown to the audience during recording (well, they were a luxury item in those days) one was returned hitting the usually ever calm David Jacobs in the face. Radio Luxembourg had no jurisdiction over freelance directors of sponsored shows, they would never have normally allowed banana chucking. But there was always a director wanting to make a name for himself.

One young director I fondly remember was Dickie Dawson, bursting with big ideas and energy. Late one evening, just the two of us were editing in the Luxembourg Mayfair studios when the front door bell rang and Dickie said *'Oh it's probably my missus'* I went to open the door and standing there was Diana Dors. Wow! One thing I do remember, she was so much more beautiful than any photographs or film appearances I had seen. Later, we went over to the pub in Shepherds Market where Diana had conversations with some of the 'ladies of the night'. Diana was a charming, easy going, gorgeous lady with absolutely no side.

In 1959 the advent of legal commercial radio was looming and television was stealing audience numbers. Driving around the country every weekend was getting tedious. My feet were getting itchy!

The Hughie Green Radio Luxembourg quiz programmes were recorded at various locations all over the country. After an overnight in a local hotel we would set up the gear before lunch. Later, Hughie and his manager would check the dressing room and the layout of the stage. During this walk-through, Hughie would whisper into the microphone *'Can you hear me?'* to his manager in the auditorium. The manager, standing at the rear of the auditorium, usually replied *'No, I can't'*. We had long stopped enquiring how the manager heard the question. Hughie would then stare at us and make one of his faces.

On one auspicious occasion, Hughie Green, promised to get me sacked because I failed to turn the house PA up high enough. We had already told him, on previous occasions, that house PA was not our responsibility and that local companies or the house sound staff took over that job. But Hughie's memory was of the same length as his fuse! Like many artistes the volume of the public address was an important factor.

Colin Eldred and I did the series all around the country. The audiences unfailingly loved Hughie. He had an aura that connected with ordinary people. We found him to be a grumpy, unhappy person. However, he always seemed to cheer up when selecting girl hostesses for each programme series. They had to be good looking (*it was radio!*).

I had a much later experience concerning PA for a Special featuring the music of Andrew Lloyd-Webber. During an afternoon break in rehearsals, Mr. Lloyd Webber approached me and complained that one of his two lady singers were unhappy. Her PA sound was much quieter than the other. I took the opportunity to point him in the direction of the theatre house PA guy.

On being appraised of the situation, the sound guy forcefully, and rather loudly, told Mr. Lloyd-Webber that one was on a hand mike (very loud) while the other had a mike stuffed down her dress (very quiet). He explained that the distance between the microphone and the source of sound was an important one and that was the source of the problem Mr. Lloyd-Webber, didn't appear to grasp this and further reiterated his complaint. The sound guy did ditto without fear, standing his ground proudly. I gloated in the far corner. Why couldn't I be more like that?

A bad case of PA blues was a David Frost pilot, a sort of political 'quiz show' before an audience at the

Limehouse Television Studios. He insisted on such a high level of PA that it was constantly on the verge of howling. Before recording, and in front of the audience, he let me know that if the volume was turned down he would stop the show. He said something like' 'If you are listening Mr. Soundman, I will stop talking if I hear any reduction in the house PA'.

If you are listening? Did he imagine I was doing a crossword puzzle? After this statement and just as we were about to go in to record, the producer came into sound control and whispered to me, *'don't worry, this show will never go out.'* I still wonder how a clever, and highly successful, person like David Frost could stand performing before an audience with the public address whistling.

Colin Eldred was at Luxembourg before my arrival and stayed long after I had left. He later joined *Anglia Television* as a very successful TV Director. Colin married Jean, a production assistant for EMI records (Beecher-Stevens PA) when we were doing the dee jay shows. Jean organized the running order, timed the programmes and did all the paperwork for EMI, another task that would be shared by at least two some years later.

Boredom was creeping in, time to move on. The television scene was expanding rapidly, perhaps I could get a job? This time I would try to do it by myself without dad's aid. I applied at Associated Television (ATV) eventually being interviewed by Head of Sound, Ray McCabe (probably the coolest sound guy I have ever known, although Jim Willis, Head of Sound when I joined Luxembourg would have contested that title). I remember Ray McCabe being even more nervous than me during that interview. He never asked me my age, or schooling. Just concerned with my experience. That certainly wouldn't happen today.

Four weeks later I was staring at Primo Scala and his Accordion band through the Radio Luxembourg control room window of Studio A. The microphones in the studio were sticking up like Triffids amidst accordions in full gallop. Suddenly, the phone flashed, incoming call, I muted the loudspeakers and Ray McCabe's secretary (Barbara Williams) asked me if I could start as soon as possible.

Six years and several promotions later, I was a Senior Sound Director at ATV, the finest television production company in the world. Never generous with praise, I think that dad finally admitted I had 'found' a trade. Although 'famous names' usually washed over dad's head he did light up when I told him I was doing a Bing Crosby Christmas Show. Dad often 'crooned' like Bing – I don't have a recording of that, best left to the memory bank.

I had badly misjudged the demise of Radio Luxembourg by many, many years. Despite the advent of commercial radio in Great Britain and the ever growing monster of television channels gobbling up the viewing figures, Radio Luxembourg lasted for years. Several times I returned to Hertford Street. Pat was still in reception with her billowing skirts. Richard Milliard from the BBC had taken my job. Colin Eldred and the other guys were still at it but the producers had changed. Then the office staff got more 'modern' and with it. Then, one day . . . even Pat had gone. I got past the new receptionist and went downstairs to the editing suites and not a soul did I recognize. An era had passed.
But, I am still pleased I made the break into television sound when I did. I missed the closeness of Hertford Street, where everybody knew everybody and we all lived in each other's pockets. Happy days, but gone. However, don't despair, there may well be more 'Luxembourg' anecdotes later.

***

6. ATV the Light Entertainment Factory.

FROM THE EARLY 1960's and onwards, the Associated Television studios at Boreham Wood (Elstree) in Hertfordshire became the Mecca for dozens of American production series. The facilities and technical expertise of the staff surpassed any other television studio, especially in the musical production field. I write this with confidence despite the brilliant work done by the London Weekend Television (LWT) sound department, more of which later.

Top American stars of stage and screen were regular visitors to Elstree. Musical Specials and top class drama poured out. This commitment was added to the myriad of programming that ATV turned out to satisfy their franchise agreement.

In the very beginning, stars like Jo Stafford, Carol Channing, Lena Horne, Sammy Davis Jr. Fred McMurray, Glenn Campbell, Tennessee Ernie Ford and Burt Bacharach filled the two larger studios. Music emitted from Studio D Band Room at all times of the night and day.

This cacophony of top quality programming would continue until the early eighties when the Muppet Shows finally finished their fifth year and the production arm of the studios was compelled to move to Nottingham in the East Midlands of England in a political re-working of the license renewals.

In 1984 the studios were taken over by the BBC and extensively used. *East Enders* emanates from the back lot on the very same ground where ATV's *Honey Lane* was made (an earlier East Enders). Not to mention *Clayhanger, Auf Weidersehen Pet, The Bing Crosby 1976 Christmas Show and Shakespeare* also heavily reliant on that back lot. Latest up-date on the ex-ATV site (2018) is that re-building of facilities is at full steam ahead. The *East Enders* back lot is being totally re-built for the advent of digital television. The old sets seen through the 'new' system look tacky. The street may be split into two to allow continuous shooting. Obviously faith in the series is at maximum at the beeb!

New buildings are replacing car parks so that staff often have to park off-site. Apparently, a local council site has been procured to fill this gap, so staff don't have to search around.

However, long before this occurred, ATV lost its weekend London transmission franchise in 1968 but increased the Midlands to seven days a week. This action prompted Lord Lew Grade to retain the Elstree site to continue making programmes for the Midland franchise whilst increasing the drive for the American and worldwide export market where an influx of world-class entertainers and film stars started to arrive.

I joined ATV as a trainee on £10 pw. Being used to six-seven days a week schedule at Radio Luxembourg, I was astounded to learn my first week at ATV would be scheduled to Tuesday and Friday. Saturday and Sunday were my 'notional' days off! What did Monday, Wednesday and Thursday constitute then? Tuesday I was to report to the ATV Highbury studios at 1400 hours for a live transmission of *Emergency Ward 10.*

I arrived early. Place deserted - found the sound control room. Good Lord, there is a motorbike in pieces on the floor and a worried gentlemen. It's Jim Gravina, he had had an accident en route to work and was disassembling then assembling the wheels of his machine. Covered in grease we shook hands. (Jim relocated to Townsville in Australia in the sixties. We still keep in touch). Sound Director, Dennis Bassinger has taken the day off, Peter Hubbard, his number two is mixing the show, so the crew is one short – hence me! After lunch the crew assembled. I am given the task of tracking two booms on tonight's edition of *Emergency Ward 10.* First question . . . what does tracking mean and secondly, what the hell is a boom? The crew gather on the floor while the director (Peter Sasdy, a Hungarian refugee from 1956) walks and talks us through the action without the artistes. His accent is strong.

There are two booms covering the sound pick-up. They will traverse from set to set with head-phoned operators aloft as the rehearsal goes on. I will move them to different chalk marks in different sets as the action dictates. Confused and head going round in circles, I achieve this but only with the help of camera trackers, Gerry Whitney and Peter Thierry. Thank you guys, I shall never forget that help you freely gave me.

The afternoon is spent blocking the action for sound and cameras. This is a rough rehearsal followed by the 'dress run' which is sacrosanct and ends sharp at six. One hour meal break, then half hour for line-up where vision control tweak the three cameras and lines to Foley Street, the transmission hub, are checked and carried out.

I spend the time sitting in my car in a daze, wish I hadn't worn a posh suit. On the night, I get through it. Couple of dodgy moments but *'what the hay'* live is live. It's history. After transmission a friendly drink in the nearby pub where shots are discussed, *'If only the director had taken me earlier . . .'* from an unhappy cameraman. *'Don's always late when I shout up boom'* the vision mixer tells us. Other discussions range from camera angles, late cuts, too much crabbing and unnecessary pups – all jargon I will get used to and continue the myth of using. Television people have a vocabulary of about 100 words. Not many refer to real life . . . I'm kidding!

For the aficionados;
'What the hay' derived the thirties when censorship in Hollywood was introduced by the Hays Office. This almost draconian organization, designed originally to ban flimsy dresses and scenes of a sexual nature (of which many were increasingly being shown) also started to affect scripts. Unable to no longer say 'what the hell . . .' artistes and comedians said 'what the hay'. All that seems to have gone by the board these days as American crime series expound considerably broader dialogue than 'what the hay'.

Oh how I long for the days of Jack Benny, Bob Hope and a myriad of other entertainments who were able to entertain us with slick gags and routines without the need for smut or, increasing lately, extremely bad language. Morecambe & Wise, Des O'Connor, Arthur Haynes and dozens of brilliant sit-coms never went the cheap route. The so-called 'watershed' hour of nine o'clock assuming all the kiddie winkies have gone to slumber are so out of date. They are probably all checking out the internet in their bedrooms under the eiderdown. The price we pay for progress.

***

7. The Liberace Specials.

AFTER A LONG RUNNING hit series in the USA and straight from a European tour, Liberace arrived at Elstree to record ten one hour Specials for NBC. Despite jokey early derision, he quickly won over everybody with his geniality and sheer professionalism. From a sound perspective, he was a joy to work with.

I am now a Sound Director, one of seven. Four in the studio and three covering outside broadcasts. My music sound mixing experience has paid off bigtime.

The middle part of the Liberace hour show was the Concert Spot. With a sixty-piece orchestra behind his special personalised Baldwin piano, Lee, dressed in one of his famous heavy brocade glittering suits would proceed to play any one of the popular classics before four cameras almost invariably in one take. Interestingly, I never saw classically-trained Liberace read a note of music throughout the three months on site.

Three concert spots of approximately twenty minutes each were recorded in one short day to avoid the set having to be erected every week. The specially made Baldwin piano was something that Liberace was proud of. He enjoyed telling his audiences that there were only two in the whole world . . . and he had both of them.

For the aficionados;
The concert spot orchestra took up most of the floor of studio C. A beautiful set with the floor transformed into a miniature concert hall.

I arranged the layout of the orchestra in conjunction with the designer and lighting director. Important to take acoustics and visual presentation equally into account. Something like 34 microphones would employed for the orchestra. All microphone stands to be at smartly angled with cables neatly affixed to the stand. Wrapping cables untidily around microphone stands was never a runner on my shows.

Liberace's beautiful Baldwin piano fronted the orchestra. I wanted no microphones to be seen. I hid two M59 condenser microphones covering the top and middle of the huge instrument. Deep at the rear, a Neumann condensor, also unseen, looked up at the piano lid, which acts as a sound board (as it was designed to).

When these three microphones were faded up alone, the sixty-piece orchestra could barely be heard through them. Totally unseen in shot, all the cabling came out of the bottom end of the instrument down the hidden back leg and with the complicity of the design department disappeared under the rostrum floor. Completely disguised. Perhaps some sound bloke somewhere would say 'where the hell are the mics?' I hope so, that what I was aiming for, that and a distinctive sound as well.

After the very first concert spot recording, Lee was invited up to sound control for a replay. The brocade suits were very heavy and even the walk up the sound stairs was arduous. My sound console was a hundred-channel Rupert Neve desk. To reach both ends of the desk, a sliding chair had been installed on a six-foot track.

When playing back the first concert spot, Lee sat in this chair and after joyfully sliding himself from side to side, greatly admired the desk, likening it to a Boeing 747 flight deck. I remarked that there were only two one 100 channel desks in the whole world, and he quickly interrupted saying;

'I know, and you've got both of them'.

He beat me to it. His laughter was infectious.

At one point, he had made a slight error in a Paganini piece (I think?). Director Colin Clewes asked him if he wanted a re-take, he replied, after a pause;

'No, I think I'll quit while I'm ahead.'

I had given his piano a very sharp top end sound, which he commented on and admired.

'Especially' he remarked *'as I can't see any microphones'* (so, he noticed?).

The shows were recorded on a Thursday evening before an audience. Lee would always address them before, during and after recording. They were mostly ardent fans and devoured his every word, admiring his diamond rings and costumes.

After the show finished and was cleared by VTR, he would thank the audience for their patience during the scene breaks and tell them how much he admired the guest star's performance, often sharing a little private story about them, but never detrimental. He would then tell them that the only part of the show they hadn't seen was the Concert Spot - which, for technical reasons, they had to record earlier . . .'*but I could play it for you now if you wanted*'. They wanted.

He would return to the home base set furnished with an ordinary baby grand and, without orchestra, play the piece all through. On any other show, the floor crew, would be tearing the set down at this juncture, the lighting crew would be noisily working their lighting tracks and generally the studio would be dark in twenty minutes – in short . . .a wrap. But no, all the floor crew watched dutifully whilst Lee played the entire piece, after which they joined in with the applause just as heartily as the audience.

I can think of no other show, no other artiste where this would have occurred. Liberace had won the hearts and minds of everybody at ATV Elstree, just as he had, surely, around the world.

I recently watched the film *Behind the Candelabra.* Although heavily sex-orientated, Michael Douglas was super, his piano miming was perfect. Terrific make-up for both him and Matt Damon. I think Lee would have been quite chuffed, they used virtually all of his furniture and props which, apparently, were rented from Carol Channing's Hollywood house.

The shows were edited over the weekend. On Monday mornings, before rehearsals started for the next show Lee was invited up to the gallery to watch last week's finalised edit. He would sit with his eyes glued to the screen, as if seeing it, and himself for the first time. When introducing the guest star, he would often turn and say something like *'Oh I really like her'*. It was always apparent that he enjoyed watching the show just as much as starring in it.

During the rehearsal of one show, I tried to raise my sound guys (John Clark and John Segal) on the floor because a minor problem had occurred up-stage where the guest star was rehearsing. Having no success on talkback I dashed down the stairs to find both of them sitting in the darkened Liberace home base set having a quiet discussion with Lee. I jokingly admonished them and they tore up-stage quickly to sort out a snag with a foldback speaker. Ten minutes later, Lee crept quietly into my control room and apologized for upsetting the routine of my crew. He assured me it wouldn't happen again despite my trying to convince him that there was no problem.

After the delightful experience of working on The Liberace Show we were all invited to Madame Tussauds in London where Lee had organized a big party for everybody. All the guests were invited to bring a partner, an unusual occurrence for conventional wrap parties. Many of the guest stars still in the country also showed up. At the entrance of the venue, Lee would be standing with his mother who had flown over for this event. He gleefully introduced her to virtually everybody as they arrived;

'Mom, this is Teddie'
'Hi Teddie'
'He did the audio'
'Oh'
'He did it good Mom'
(Pause)
'He'd better'

During that memorable evening where wine and goodwill flowed, Lee managed to take his mom round to just about everybody there. Something like 250 people, giving as much time to, say, a lighting console operator and his wife as Lord and Lady Lew Grade, who were also present.

Producer/Director Colin Clewes and his wife Joy had just been presented with a baby boy. They named him Lee, and Liberace happily became the Godfather. I can think of no nicer guy, no more talented an entertainer than Liberace and I wish that we could all see, and enjoy, programmes of this stature again.

***

8. Emergency Ward 10 to Nat King Cole.

BECAUSE ATV WAS in cahoots with a consortium of powerful impresarios it followed that to fill the screen with hours of top quality programming was not a logistic problem. These impresarios owned theatres and had control of a vast army of performers through their talent agencies. Even as early as 1955, light entertainment and ATV became synonymous.

The *Saturday Spectacular* live transmissions from The Wood Green Empire set the scene from Independent Television's inception. How well I remember rigging the band early on a Saturday morning when a young girl and her mother came into the studio looking for make-up. We wondered why a new make-up girl would bring her mum. Later, on camera rehearsal that little girl turned to be the glorious Janette Scott and her mum was Thora Hird.

The Alma Cogan Show emanated from the Hackney Empire. Once again at 8am, lights were noisily being moved. Trucks were delivering sets. Scene shifters swarmed around and general chaos appeared to be the order of the day. Twelve hours later, the glamourous Alma Cogan would front a polished show that you would have thought took days to prepare.

Emergency Ward Ten went out live twice a week from the Highbury Studios. After tracking booms for many months I was finally let loose on a Ward 10 boom. In the beginning (in my innocence) I thought the surgeons and doctors were actually real, the acting was so good.

I recollect one occasion when a consultant had a long interview in a side set. I followed the dialogue with my script and, to my horror, the consultant jumped three pages and gave the other actor the final pay-off line to the scene. She reacted without showing too much surprised and the director was left with three cameras in the office looking at two blank faces whilst the floor manager was waiting to cue the actors in a different set, some twenty five yards away. Unable to cut away, one camera dashed for the new set showing flashing acres of floor en route whereupon the next scene took place.

That's live television for you.

Another 'live' occasion. An afternoon children's drama programme. Three kids are on top of a castle looking out for the arrival of two people on horseback. The horsemen footage had been pre-recorded on film in eight segments. These would be run in to fit in with the kid's dialogue on the castle roof (in the studio, of course). The director (who shall remain nameless) cued telecine for the first three items, then, not noticed by the director, the telecine operator had inadvertently run through one short item. Thus, when the net item was cued it was totally out of sync with the script. This went on for a couple of minutes making no sense to anybody.

After the transmission, the said director buried his head in his hands and was heard to moan; *'I wish I was dead'*. Oh! The joys of live television.

Part two of a serious drama is in progress live from Wood Green Studios.

All three cameras are covering the lengthy scene. Towards the end, camera three (I think it was Keith Farthing?) is released to be ready to start the following scene. Because Wood Green was not strictly a drama studio, the next scene could only be reached by pushing the camera behind the cyclorama, in one end and out the other. Some fifty feet. This will be performed quietly as the action still going on is dramatic and intense.

Halfway through this manoeuvre the camera cable gets caught up with some stage weights and in trying to release it the cable disengages itself from the camera. This will now involve vision control some twenty minutes to realign the machine. Being cut off from the world, the cameraman has no way of informing the control room. His cut-off cable has also cut off talkback.

Slight panic in the control room as the camera expected at the next scene is now showing a blank screen. The director requests an explanation. None is given because none is known. The moment for action in the next scene has arrived and the actors seeing no camera are hesitant to commence the scene . . . well, need I go on. The director ages ten years and eventually the transmission goes dark. People at home are slightly puzzled. Is it their aerial on the blink again? Whatever. Time to make a cup of tea.

My favourite live telly story is one I mentioned earlier. A well-known pop singer was to appear on a live evening show extolling the virtues of his latest hit. He would mime to his record at the Foley Street studio where, although small and badly equipped, had the big advantage was being in the middle of London.

The sound mixer is our head of sound Ray McCabe on a very rare sortie into the realms of actual production. Ray, a terrific sound mixer was lured from the BBC. He is now head of department and takes the opportunity to get outside now and again. Quite legitimate in this case as someone has gone sick. His number two is Ray Knipe who is acting as gram operator and has recorded the track to be televised onto tape. Trying to play an actual record on a live show is fraught with problems. The needle might jump, the operator can't cue it at exactly the right time etc.

The compere is disc jockey Jack Jackson. He announces the performer and we cut to him smiling waiting for his big hit to be played. Ray cues tape. But Ray Knipe has inadvertently recorded the B side of the record. The music starts and a look of near horror wipes the smile off the singer's face. He knows it's the wrong music. He knows it's the B side, one that he hasn't bothered listening to since recording it a couple of weeks before.

The director throws a verbal fit over talkback.

'That's the wrong side Ray," He shouts at Ray McCabe over talkback.

Ray turns to Ray and says; *'Is that the wrong side, Ray?'*

Ray stares at his twirling tape recorder as if **it** were to blame. He replies;

'Not to my knowledge, Ray'.

Both Rays' are very cool guys. No panic, no flapping. The director asks (in panic-stricken tone) whether it can quickly be replaced with the right side. Ray McCabe informs him, no. The record is no longer in the control room. It was transferred to tape and that cannot be altered.

The director is not happy. Actually, he wants to kill whoever is responsible. Either of the Rays' will do. The artist meanwhile is miming to his unwanted track as best he can. The director who had planned a couple of crafty mixes and wipes to coincide with the music of the A side has forgotten to cut to any other camera. His planned shoot has gone up the pictures and the number finally ends with Jack Jackson hastily introducing the next item. There was a post mortem, an unusual occurrence for a live show. However nothing came of it. No paperwork existed saying which side of the record should be played.

I know all this because I was the hapless sound assistant on the studio floor listening to all the commotion on talkback. I am operating the foldback loudspeaker playing the wrong music track. The singer has looked at me as if I was responsible for the error. I took quite a bit of flak from the artist, the floor manager and probably the tea lady too. A nearby cameraman silently sniggers. This will be a good story form him to tell his compatriots.

Live television.
It's Emergency Ward Ten again. Two doctors are slowly walking down a corridor discussing how to break some very bad news to a patient's relatives. As they traverse the lengthy corridor followed by a camera, they suddenly see a Mole Richardson boom crossing their path. The boom operator, unaware of his intrusion is studying his script preparing for his next scene. Tracking the boom is, Noel Tyler. A South African sound assistant who has been at ATV since its inception. Noel stops tracking, sees the doctors, stares at them almost defying their presence before slowly pushing the boom through an aperture at the end of the corridor.

The doctors, bless them, carry on their serious and quiet conversation as if Mole Richardson booms in hospital corridors were an everyday occurrence in modern National Health Hospitals.

Some days later, Noel gets cod fan mail from wives of various employees. They know Noel of old and are not surprised at his unscheduled appearance on national television.

Lew Grade made a dreadful error when he axed Ward 10. I really think it would still be going today. There have been imitators but Ward 10 was the real McCoy.

I assume that readers will know what boom is. The earlier Mole Richardson model only moved forward or backward. The later Fisher boom, imported from the United States could go backwards, forwards and even crab sideways. And for comfort, the operator had a seat. The long-rack

Fisher boom allowed the boom to be further away from the set giving cameras more room to manoeuvre.

Both models had a script platform and sometimes a small light. Talkback to booms came from production control and, separately, the sound director. Reverse talkback to the sound director was available via a foot switch. It was inadvisable to raise your voice when using this facility.

I remember one boom operator, during a pause in the action telling the sound director that he didn't actually miss a line of dialogue, the artiste was ad libbing.

'The artiste' on overhearing this called for the microphone at the end of the boom to be available where he shouted for all to hear;
'I was not bloody ad libbing . . . I had a quick turn upstage, which was scripted and you missed the line'.

The artiste was the marvellous actor Patrick Wymark of *Planemakers* and *Power Game* fame. Poor old boom op' - very embarrassed.

Emergency Ward Ten again.
One minute before transmission. A boom operator (on sound talkback) loudly whispers to his nearby compatriot (who has the opening scene); *'Good luck, fatty.'* (This good natured taunt because of his workmate's love for bacon sandwiches). Within earshot and waiting for her opening scene, the ward sister, who, shall we say was rather voluptuous looks up at the boom operator with an accusing icy stare. If looks could kill.

Wearing headphones often means you speak too loudly. He should have kept shtum.

Regretfully, boom operating is becoming a dying art, thanks to the innovation of radio microphones and the preponderance of light entertainment and quiz type shows where a boom would be an encumbrance on the set.

Happily, most soaps are compelled to use booms. It would be an unbelievable nightmare if all the actors in

Coronation Street had to wear a personal microphone. Imagine five costume changes per drama where the hidden microphone would have to be changed and reinserted without being seen?

Perhaps in the years to come, all actors will have to be fitted with a transmitter in their throats to be picked up wherever they work. Perhaps I ought to have patented this notion some years ago? However, that would have been an even bigger disservice to boom operating.

A good boom operator is virtually sound mixing. Artistes have loud or soft voices and variance of shots dictate how they should be heard. He (or these days 'she') is avidly following a script, watching which shot has been selected and, above all, avoiding shadowing the artiste or the set.

In the early days our top boom operator at ATV (Roy Nilsen) used to be in the merchant navy. This was another art where ten A levels would be of no help. Roy would swoop in for a close-up and quickly leave before the following wide shot, often frightening the life out of the artiste and the vision mixer. The cry *'UP BOOM'* emanating from the production gallery is one every boom operator remembers, almost with affection! Any operator who doesn't regularly hear this probably wasn't a very good one.

Modern day techniques do not require this stringent type of operating. Different types of microphones allow voice pick-up to be achieved without swooping. Studio acoustics also play a big part in the ability to capture dialogue without getting the microphone too close. Different types of microphones are also available.

My first boom was on a live Sunday afternoon history lecture programme with A. J. P. Taylor. These were transmitted from Wood Green Empire on a

Sunday afternoon. In wide shot, he would walk onto the set with the opening titles superimposed, then, as the lights came up, cut to the tight shot and drop the boom in.

Then he stood still for ages, talking. While I stood still on the boom platform shaking as I followed the shots.

My first musical boom was at Hackney Empire on *The Beverley Sisters Show*. I was on secondary boom, which turned out to be the only boom because of lighting. In rehearsal, the girls would point to themselves and whisper loudly to me; *'I'm next . . .'* so I would know who to point the microphone at. The show went out live and I was in shot once, skimming the top of frame. Sound Director Dennis Bassinger was ecstatic as this showed I was as near the artistes as possible. Boom operators were quite chuffed if they 'bent' the top line, Cameramen were not so thrilled. In 405 line scanning the top three or four lines were never seen at home.

One tragic night, our head of sound, Ray McCabe mysteriously vanished after popping in at a Hackney Empire recording. He was never found and his disappearance was never solved. His souped up Mini was found on the Embankment, the driver's door ajar and no Ray McCabe. Did he feel sick and leaned over the parapet too far? Nobody knows.

To save the head of department going to an audio-unfriendly technical arm (a frightening possibility), Dennis Bassinger (my sound director) agreed to become the new head of sound which meant he could no longer be involved with hands-on production, quite a sacrifice at that time. Ray McCabe had made the same sacrifice and confided to me that he regretted it.

There is a thrill that is difficult to explain when you are mixing a big show, working two booms, other floor mikes and another forty, or so, on the orchestra. Usually, one hand hovering on the audience reaction channels because audience reaction is often more important than a flute solo. Even a hundred channel desk had its limitations. One Val Doonican show at Elstree had the band in the bandroom for most of the time before dashing out during a commercial break to appear on stage for the final Val

Doonican medley. Add the Acker Bilk band as well, I used up something like eighty-odd microphone channels. They weren't all like this.

So, guys like Dennis and Ray and many other in the television world gave up that thrill to sit behind a desk, arrange schedules and answer questions from even higher management. Later however, Dennis Bassinger became head of everything at ATV. As a small point of interest; Dennis, as a motor cycle rider lost an eye in the dying day of the war. Despite this encumbrance, he was a superb (crazy) driver, as was Ray McCabe.

Ray Knipe, the number 2 on my crew (crew 4) was an avid rally enthusiast. He once talked me into entering an ATV rally traversing the lanes and by-ways of Hertfordshire. My trusty and much loved MG Magnette was to be used with Ray being my co-driver and map reader.

The course was in a maze of Hertfordshire country lanes. Dusk had fallen and as Ray nonchalantly consulted his map he suddenly advised me to make a sharp left. I did. Entering a field at 45mph through an open farm gate. We sunk in two feet of mud and eventually a tractor had to extract us. Ray's calmness at the scene of the catastrophe is summed up by his often used utterance *'I'm agog with indifference'*. I found clogged mud under my car weeks after the event. Vision mixer, Mary Forrest, won that race and many others.

Inexplicably, ALL the sound guys (and Judi Headman) at Limehouse Television (in the eighties) were equally crazy drivers. Sharing a car with Chris Blake on the ninety minute drive to Limehouse Studios in London's Docklands, Chris often frightened the life out of me. I once suggested I should sit in the passenger seat in apparent distress having my head bandaged with blood seeping as an excuse for his mad driving to reach the nearest hospital. Needless to say, I am the epitome of courtesy on the roads!

A huge production at Wood Green Empire was the Nat King Cole Show. He was appearing at that year's Royal Variety Show and we, at the Wood Green studio, were waiting for him to record a Special with virtually no rehearsal.

There were three sets, London, Paris and Rome. The London set was a park. The orchestra pit was filled with benches and foliage where lovers roamed while Nat sang on the bridge built over the pit. Paris was an Eiffel Tower backdrop where the orchestra pit now became a jazz night club introducing Nat's famous trio. Rome was a canal sequence with the pit now filled with water. This mammoth enterprise took three scene crews to operate the set changes all under the auspices of the brilliant designer, Jon Scoffield. It was directed by head honcho Bill Ward, who never showed until 'the night' because he was directing the Royal Variety.

Dennis Bassinger, my sound director gave me the task of operating the fold back speaker, through which Nat would hear the band under the baton of Jack Parnell, all safely ensconced in the bandroom situated under the Royal circle. This huge box was on wheels, it contained a bomb-proof amplifier that could blast the auditorium if need be with a hefty sixteen inch loudspeaker. With my controlling the volume it allowed me to roam the floor as near to Nat as possible without being in shot. For any extra quiet orchestra portions, I could increase the volume slightly.

Only one camera on a huge crane was used, operated by ace senior cameraman, Johnny Glenister. The floor manager (the legendary Billy Glaze) crouched alongside the crane pointing Nat King Cole to his next mark as the show progressed. He was on a radio microphone. The orchestra level emanating from the loudspeaker had to be kept low so as not to 'colour' the sound. Nat's voice was naturally quiet thus his microphone had to be wound quite high and would risk hearing the orchestra played back through the foldback speaker if it were faded up too much. Years later, as a sound director, I began to appreciate the efforts of a good foldback speaker operator. Not a menial task, by any means.

It all looked so smooth considering there was no rehearsal. I had friends in the audience who had never been to a television show before. They marvelled at the quantity of people it took to make what appeared on the screen such a simple thing. It took about forty minutes for the set changes, which my friends found just as fascinating as the show itself. I hope they didn't think all programmes were as complex.

My friend's wife was even more intrigued with the sight of Jon Scoffield, our young, talented and extremely handsome designer nonchalantly strolling the studio floor directing the set changes. Head of Light Entertainment, Bill Ward was busy directing the Royal Variety Show that year at the London Palladium. He allowed Jon Scoffield to 'direct' the Nat King Show rehearsals in his absence. Jon, was later to become one of the finest light entertainment directors ever.

It was a very successful show, love to see it again, and where is that videotape? I've searched YouTube. Mr Cole, possibly realizing the importance of keeping the foldback at a low level, came up to me afterwards and thanked me. I guess we were so close to each other for a whole day and he got to recognize me behind the huge, wheeled box?

The foldback speaker at a live Saturday Spectacular will be forever on the minds of Nina & Frederick at Wood Green Empire. Their hit song *Listen to the Ocean* was somewhat marred by Sound Director Des Gray forgetting to punch the orchestra to foldback. He had been checking something with Jack's band during a commercial break and had taken the feed off foldback to the artistes on the floor. During which period the audience were being entertained by the warm-up guy.

When part three started, Nina & Frederick were introduced and their music started. Trouble was, they couldn't hear it. I turned the volume up to maximum as I could hear the orchestra very faintly. They struggled for a few bars until Des, in sound control, suddenly realized he had turned the foldback feed off. As he punched the button to restore the feed, the sound burst from the loudspeaker like an exploding bomb. Nina & Fredrick visibly jumped a foot in the air. I quickly restored the volume to normal and they got through to the end.

Live television again, full of surprises.

One Roy Castle Show, also from Wood Green Empire was transmitted live directed by Colin Clewes, also using only one camera with Johnny Glenister on a Mole crane. This time, booms and stand microphones were employed.

The ATV logo had been painted onto the studio floor and on transmission, Johnny, in his viewfinder, saw the ATV logo being rolled live from telecine. He then had a couple of seconds to match it up on the floor painted logo. When he had achieved this, the vision mixer mixed from telecine to camera one and as Johnny pulled out, Roy Castle's legs entered shot dancing for the first musical item, very innovative at the time, long before the days of blue screen.

This was a Colin Clewes special. I did dozens of light entertainment shows for Colin. He came from the BBC as a famed senior cameraman and became an even more famed director. Seventeen Engelbert Humperdinck shows would have remained on his, and my, mind for ever!

SUNDAY NIGHT AT THE LONDON PALLADIUM was probably the finest light entertainment spectacle to come from ATV, running for years with the highest viewing figures possible. The show made stars of several comperes from Tommy Trinder onwards.

The name Bruce Forsyth is forever linked with the Palladium. I was fortunate to work on many of Bruce's'

Specials. One in particular aimed at the American market also starred Rita Moreno (from the West Side Story movie). One lengthy item called My Dark Lady was rehearsed extensively up to shooting stage before it was discovered that copyright clearance from the authors of 'My **fair** Lady' hadn't been achieved. Another item was hastily written and shot. Both Bruce and Rita taking it in their stride. Bruce had a massively long career culminating in '*Strictly come Dancing*', but his Palladium days will remain firmly lodged in many people's memories.

It was imperative that this flagship programme should only be trusted in the hands of the top-of-the-tree staff. Sound-wise, only Dennis Bassinger and Bill Nuttall were permitted to work it. In the beginning, the sound crew started very early morning with the rig. This involved forty, or more, microphones and associated stands and cabling for the pit orchestra plus all the stage requirements. If the orchestra had to appear on stage, as often happened, the number of microphones, stands and cabling was virtually doubled.

Camera positions were similar for most shows. Two cameras were static in the rear of the stalls. Other cameras were either side of the proscenium arch or roaming the floor. A camera in the royal circle was also deployed. Camera requirements were dictated by the director and often switched around to suit the content of the show. After lunch, a camera rehearsal where shots were plotted and finalised was followed by a tea break and the dress rehearsal, which was considered sacrosanct.

The outside broadcast riggers, usually only involved with sporting events were responsible for the installation of all cabling, which was a considerable task. The Palladium always had a show of some sort running and the sets and equipment for this had to be cleared on the Saturday night ready for the riggers. If cameras required tracking (moving a camera while it was on shot), for some obscure reason, this was also a riggers job. Something that studio camera trackers were baffled by.

While ATV held the London franchise, the Palladium was staffed and equipped by the Elstree studios. After some years, it was decided to split the sound crew into two. Crew one would arrive at 6.30am get everything rigged for the 1030 bandcall before handing over to the second crew who saw the show through and de-rigged.

A sound truck was parked alongside the production control room and other ATV vehicles in Ramilles Place at the rear of the Palladium by the stage door. It was a state-of-the-art truck with super mixing facilities. Lines from the stage and orchestra pit were fed to the sound truck via a complicated method.

The plugging of these microphones and various talkback lines was a mystery to many. Microphone input points in the wings or on stage were identified as one thing going under the stage and re-labelled as something else and then out to the little room backing onto Ramilles Place where the sound truck was parked. For an example; the main riser microphone (the one centre stage) plugged into G4 on stage, LL3 under the pit, GF2 in Ramilles Place then to the main bay in the sound truck as C7 and finally sub-mix channel 16. These numbers are fictitious but, multiply by another fifty microphones, give an inkling of the complexity. There was a plugging list made up the day before when the requirement were known. If the senior rigging sound guy lost this list (it happened twice) it was nothing short of a calamity.

The sound director and his number two arrived around 8.30 am and if sound directors Bill Nuttall or Dennis Bassinger couldn't walk into the sound truck and successfully fade up the band channels, heads would roll.

When I became a number two on the crew, I was designated fit to supervise this early morning rig. I was shaky on technical plugging but Guy Caplin, my assistant, assured me it was a doddle and not to worry about it. We rigged all the band microphones and Guy plugged up the truck. When I went to the desk to check the feeds I got nothing but hiss. No sound coming from anywhere. Guy was equally puzzled, convinced he had plugged up correctly. Heads were being scratched.

Panic stations. Bill Nuttall was due in twenty minutes. I would be dead in the water. Suddenly, Bill's number two, Len Penfold, showed up early. I quickly explained the problem. He stared at Guy, pushed him aside and within five minutes had the plugging pulled out and reinstated correctly. Something like fifty or sixty short cables re-plugged, all from memory.

When band call and artiste walk-through started around 1030 am we could usually take a breather, watching the rehearsals was always fun. Tommy Cooper, describing his act to the director in the morning rehearsal was often funnier than his real act on the night. He'd get his props all mixed up and seemed genuinely baffled. That's the way it seemed to us.

Being in the wings on the night was always interesting. To see Johnny Hart, the magician, taking playing cards out of thin air, not meant to be seen from the side. Another magician made a dove disappear before your very eyes – actually it was thrown into the tails of his evening dress. Once, he missed and the dove went up-stage at a rate of knots. Like that Monty Python parrot, it was definitely dead!

When the band was required to be on stage for a singing star finale, it was usually chaotic, a four minute commercial break was often the time allotted and there would still be much backstage noise as Bruce Forsyth introduced the top of the bill.

The musicians would be struggling to get out of the pit and onto the stage clutching their instruments to safeguard them in the melee. Electricians would push and shove to get the music stand lights working while stage hands handled the actually music stands. You can imagine the scene with two sound guys jostling amidst all this before placing twenty or more microphone stands, everybody convinced their task was the more important.

On one occasion, in the wings, comrade Dave Millard and I had to page the loom of orchestra sound cables as the band started to revolve as Bruce, just back from commercial break was ad-libbing to fill time, finally got the nod to introduce the top of the bill. Suddenly, to our horror, the loom got jammed in the revolve gap and Dave tried to pull it out without success. He was heading for the front of house when I grabbed his legs and gave a massive tug just before he started to appear on the proscenium side as Shirley Bassey was entering from the opposite side.

Sound-wise, those early days were often terrifying. One lady singer Miss Eileen Cochrane was unhappy with her sound treatment. A microphone had gone down on the night and the head of sound was virtually threatened that it could *NEVER* happen again. Apparently, that top ATV Executive was a . . . personal friend of Miss Cochrane. When she next appeared it might be assumed that head of sound, Ray McCabe would be sitting at home biting his finger nails and hoping nothing went wrong. Actually, I doubt that's true. Ray was probably outside tuning up his souped up Mini. *'Agog with indifference'* could also be applied to Ray.

Years later, owing to union edicts, the Palladium crewing had to originate from the Birmingham studios. At this time I was to sound direct a Royal Variety Palladium Special designed for the American market. It was to be produced by the magical team of Gary Smith and Dwight Hemion. They were the first choice for every American star from Barbra Streisand to Elvis Presley via Frank Sinatra and Bing Crosby.
Once more, unionism ordained that I would not be allowed to sit in the Birmingham sound truck or take any part in the mixing process. However, it had already been arranged that I would re-mix in Los Angeles, where director Dwight Hemion would be editing the final show.

I attended the rehearsals in the theatre itself ensuring that all the microphones and channels in use were going to sixteen track while the Birmingham crews worked the show. I recollect one act required some railway train effects. These I found in the Elstree sound library at 7 am before travelling on to the Palladium for the rehearsal and performance.

I had little jurisdiction over microphone choice. The house public address system favoured the heavy ribbon microphone as usually seen on rock groups. Large mikes with big black windshields etc were not my idea of a sophisticated stage microphone. I managed to win this round except in the case of Julie Andrews who was persuaded by the house PA that the 'big, black microphone' would give her better pick-up in the theatre. I pleaded that twenty million viewers were more important than the theatre audience, but to no avail. Her performance, often marred by 'pops', went out in the States without treatment.

We had hired the *Rolling Stones* sound truck to copy all the sound tapes to take to LA, while the masters would stay in England for the British version. After the programme finished near midnight, there was the usual booze-up in the green room. But, I had other fish to fry. The Rolling Stones guys were quite used to all night shoots so we worked all night.

Next morning I had a cab laid on by ATV to take me back to Elstree. En route the cab driver had to pick up Lynette Davies, the gorgeous star of *The Foundation* drama series being made at that time. The driver, after leaving the Palladium headed in the wrong direction towards the Thames. I asked him where he was going and he said Er . . . Elstree. He had no idea of the route, telling me he was actually an airline pilot freelancing the cab business.

I managed to get him to the address in north London to pick up Lynette for her early morning make-up call at Elstree. She looked just as gorgeous at 7 am as she did on the show. I hope that cabbie got his directions right when he returned to flying. Where do they get these guys?

I had the pleasure of working on several episodes of the *Foundation* directed by John Cooper, another talented ATV stalwart. But for my ongoing commitment on the Muppets, I would have loved doing John's later series *sounding Brass*, featuring lots of brass bands. This programme went to Peter Wernham, who was also head of dubbing and the sound effects department. I saw a couple of episodes; really good. Why, oh, why are these lovely dramas never to be seen again?

Five hours after that cab finally got to Elstree I was in a 747 headed for LA. Billy Glaze, now production manager for Gary and Dwight had possession of the videotape masters. Billy had flown the Atlantic dozens of times in that role and, like most, frequent flyers, was not a good passenger, convinced this was one flight to many etc. Shortly after take-off Billy called the stewardess and complained about a squeaking noise coming from the airframe. She calmed him down with a vodka and tonic; *'Don't worry about it, Billy, it always makes that noise'*. Billy was a known factor on transatlantic flights. More on the indefatigable Billy Glaze (brother of Peter Glaze from *Crackerjack*) later.

    For three days and nights Dwight Hemion edited the show sending me the finished video chunks to my studio on Sunset, where I was able to go to the original sixteen tracks and re-mix to match Dwight's version of the two hour special. The time flashed by before, after many all-night sessions, I returned home via San Francisco where I slept in the *Holiday Inn* for sixteen solid hours.

Two days later, a cabbie in New York asked me what I was doing there, I told him about the show which had aired the night before. He said; *'Jeeze that guy with the fez was sure something'*. Despite all the top stars, Julie Andrews, Shirley MacLaine, Johnny Dankworth and his orchestra with Cleo Laine, and many others, Tommy Cooper still got the headlines.

For another Palladium Special, Bob Hope played an impresario while Raquel Welch, in a shimmering gown, rose from below stage on the circular lift, more used in pantomimes. (Wow! I still recollect that!). This production was directed by Jon Scoffield. The scenery was built in the Birmingham studios before being transported to London where it was discovered they had transposed measurements in feet to metres. A lot of chain sawing went on and we started five hours late. Jon appeared unperturbed.

For this programme we would pre-record many of the songs at Elstree. Something the Birmingham crew were unable to do. Raquel Welch arrived late at night in the band room to record her vocal track. After a couple of takes she appeared to be happy. On talkback I enquired whether she would like to hear it played back in the vocal booth and she told my sound guy that she wanted to come up to the control room to listen to it. Panic stations. Our control room was in its usual mess. It took five minutes to walk from the band room to sound D control. We hastily emptied ash trays, and hid half consumed bacon sandwiches. Dave McNally, my Aussie number two, even went to the extent of combing his hair and having a hasty electric shave.

When she arrived, we were almost ship-shape. Raquel Welch was not just a star; she *looked* like a star, statuesque and quite beautiful. She sat in my sliding chair and we played the track back after which I spluttered that it wasn't a final mix and I could put more echo on. She stood up and said to me *'Leave it just the way it is, Mr. Soundman, I like it'*. With that she left. Dave McNally was still in a daze – come to think of it, so was I.

It was not possible to 'leave it just the way it is' – when all the musical items were recorded I went for a re-mix on the lot. If I had them today, I would probably re-mix them again. That's sound mixing for you. Perfection achieved, then achieved again.

***

9. EARLY DAYS. Sit-coms to the super Yanks.

WHEN THE HIGHBURY STUDIOS CLOSED, Wood Green and Hackney Empire theatres were similarly abandoned and the old British National film studios at Boreham Wood (which we called Elstree!) became the headquarters with the installation of the finest lighting grids and studio equipment that money could buy.

An early studio comedy was the Arthur Haynes Show. Arthur's side-kick was Nicholas Parsons, always referred to by Arthur as 'Nickle-arse'. Rita Webb, a buxom comedienne of the period was also a regular member of the cast. I well remember her sitting in the audience during rehearsals thoroughly enjoying the show. One sketch had Mr. Parsons, acting as a policeman, about to arrest Arthur as he put up a struggle. Rita yelled from the audience area,

'*Go on Arfer, kick him in the cobblers'.*

Get a dozen Rita Webb's in the audience and you didn't need canned laughter. Arthur Haynes untimely death was a sad loss for comedy. The very first Light

Entertainment show to emanate from Elstree Studio D was Cliff Richard & the Shadows, in this series I worked on as a floor sound technician. The sound director was Bill Nuttall. I operated second boom on the first ever drama from Studio C, a live transmission called *The Man Condemned* in October 1960.

Other memorable early drama productions were; Sgt Cork; The Larkins; The Planemakers; The Power Game; Mrs Thursday; The Fraud Squad; Mainly Millicent; George & The Dragon; Pipkins; Singalong with Max Bygraves; Edward The Seventh; Father Brown; The Cedar Tree; Sapphire & Steel; Shine on Harvey Moon; Timeslip; The Strauss Family series (7); Clayhanger (26) and many more.

Ronnie Ronalde, the bird impersonator, often guest-starred. I remembered him from Radio Luxembourg when he had a series. He was a proper gentleman, always impeccably dressed. He confided that whenever he got home, no matter the time, everything would be hung up properly, trousers in a press and horns in shoes. I bet his pyjamas were pressed daily too! I believe that Ronnie was still alive and kicking at the time of writing owning a small hotel in Australia. I hope so!

I always admired Max Bygraves choice of shoes, of which he appeared to have many. He told me he never wore a pair of shoes more than seven times a year. *'Always wear good shoes, son'* he told me. With that wardrobe of footwear, no wonder they always looked different and brand new.

Max Bygraves had magical audience appeal. He had the same 'kerb' appeal as the Birds of a Feather girls. Wherever we were filming, a crowd would gather and Max would chat as if he were the bloke next door. A rare quality that not too many stars possessed. At one Radio Luxembourg Christmas Party included a trip to the Palladium where Max Bygraves topped the bill. After being introduced, he walked to the microphone, looked to the audience and whispered;

'There's a tiny house . . .' the audience would immediately respond with the second line *'On a tiny hill . . .'* they were eating out of his hands after that.

Studios A and B concentrated mainly on soaps, situation comedies, chat shows, schools, children's and religious programmes. The two larger studios C and D were used mainly for big stage dramas and musicals. Studio D had a capacious audience area, great for musicals but not so good for drama as the air conditioning for CTF (Central Television Facilities) adjoining the audience area, was never turned off and could be heard in quiet sequences.

A huge back-lot was also available where the Shakespeare Theatre in the Round was re-created for a drama series on Will Shakespeare in 1977. For the 26 episodes of Clayhanger the back lot was transformed into a Stoke-on-Trent potteries street. Previously, Honey Lane was a market stall soap opera not unlike the present day East Enders which now occupies the same back lot.

For the Bing Crosby 1976 Christmas Show, it became Dickensian again for a sequence starring David Bowie, Stanley Baxter, Ron Moody and Twiggy. This Christmas show also starred David Bowie and Ron Moody and, regretfully, was to be Bing's finale (more of this later). The last ever ATV back lot programme was the hugely successful *Auf Wiedersehen Pet* in 1983.

The Outside Broadcast units were also housed on site, usually preparing for the weekend football matches, church services, horse racing or the perennial Sunday Night at the London Palladium.

OB's were not my bailiwick but I do remember working at Goodwood. During live coverage it was never possible to hear the hoofbeats as the horses went round the huge course. The gram operator (Keith Wilkinson of OB's) had a loop of clip clops for when the horses were far away almost out of camera range. On this occasion, when the horses disappeared in the distant mist he kept the hoofbeats running gradually increasing the level as they were about to appear in the distance from the misty gloom. The hoofbeats got louder and louder, suddenly a horse finally appeared . . . just one horse! Keith slowly faded the hoofbeats. Another of the fun things about live broadcasting.

Keith kept a cushion in the scanner where the seats were not too comfortable. Some OB's went on for hours. On one of the few times I did a football match we inexplicably lost sound on transmission. The director (from Birmingham) shouted at me to restore it. Keith volunteered to go quickly to the local post office hub and find out why. He never returned. This same director, who I will describe as diminutive, once stole Keith's cushion during a commercial break while Keith had left the scanner. Ten minutes of the second half of some other football match was spent with them squabbling over the possession of the cushion. The director wanted to pull rank, Keith claimed ownership. What larks! Hope they didn't miss a goal! Incidentally, that diminutive director made it quite clear preferred proper outside broadcast crews not the blasé lot from studios. Once, on arrival at a football ground, the director saw me, turned to his PA and said;

"And what ******* shower have we got with us today?"

I told him;

"Well mate, you've done better than us".

A touch of the Elstree versus Birmingham banter there.

The ATV Elstree studios also had massive scenery workshops and storage areas. Car parking was provided for everybody. A normal day would find all four studios, editing and dubbing suites and the back lot buzzing with activity. This quantity of staff, musicians and artistes gave no problem to the ATV canteen providing sustenance sometimes sixteen hours a day throughout the entire year with self-service and waitress service facilities (and a well-attended bar!). The Muppets introduced a massive mural on the wall of the restaurant. I often wonder if it's still there.

The friendly atmosphere existing among the staff and visiting artistes at the ATV studios was of the highest nature. People literally went to work happy. At Christmas time, Lew and Kathy Grade toured the site speaking to everybody they came across before attending the legendary Christmas children's parties (I think the scene boys got more VIP coverage than anybody). For the staff, a well-paid, secure job and a good pension scheme added to the happy working environment that epitomised the true glory days of British television production. It is doubtful whether this happens anywhere today in the media, or indeed in any business. Even the mighty BBC is a shadow of its former self.

No company was as tightly run as ATV. Over-crewing was avoided by a management structure comprised mainly of ex-BBC technical people and junior management who 'knew the ropes'. Careful scheduling offered the shareholders' value for money. For a guide to this success it was generally estimated that at one time, the BBC employed more commissionaires than the entire staff of ATV Elstree!

A bit of a coup for ATV happened when VAL DOONICAN came over to us from the BBC. Massively popular, Val was given a regular weekly live extravaganza plus a series, giving him a shot at the American market. I did all of Val's shows, except one. All the ITV Doonican Shows went out live. The one I didn't do was a live outside broadcast from Warwick Castle. Being in the Midlands it had to be crewed by ATV Birmingham.

One song was pre-recorded so Val had to mime it. He was very meticulous about his miming, it was flawless. However, the pre-recorded tape was cued too early and Val found himself introducing the item while he was actually singing it. He was not a happy bunny.

The American series was aimed at the Perry Como market. Lots of donkey carts on the set appealing to the millions of Irish Americans. I think it was reasonably successful. I once commended Val on his impeccable miming, over which he took a lot of trouble. Later, we talked about the problems of live sound pick-up and general control room chat. Apparently, Val had never been in a sound production control before; he found it fascinating to such an extent that later he often had 'advice' to offer on aspects of sound mixing.

I remember putting a subtle (dare I say, haunting?) tape echo on a snare drum in a slow number. The day following the live transmission, he told me his mother-in-law was perturbed at the strange drum ticking noise and wondered whether it was a mistake. I played him the track which we had recorded on quarter inch. He listened and suggested that perhaps a slightly different echo would have been better, or perhaps more reverberation? Had he been conferring with his mother-in-law? Typical, everybody wants to be a sound mixer!

MORECAMBE & WISE came to Elstree in the sixties, also having left the comfort zone of the BBC. Colin Clewes was director and producer. The show was also designed to be seen in the USA. Apart from some strange gag structures, this involved shooting in 525 and 405 lines before the days of successful conversions. The dress run (late afternoon) was shot in 405 for the home market transmission, whilst the evening's performance was in 525 for the yanks. I believe for the first couple of shows the 405 and 525 cameras were side by side. Put a couple of booms in a set and it got crowded.

The Beatles were guest stars at one time, a hectic period where the screams of fans outside the main gates could almost be heard in the studio. Eric always addressed Ringo as 'Bongo' – I don't think it stuck. He'd be Sir Bongo now (2018). Although they enjoyed the Colin Clewes polish, I don't think the Morecambe & Wise Shows were as good as their BBC shows. Being aimed at the States, they often splashed in the middle of the Atlantic.

Jon Scoffield directed a mammoth production of *Anthony & Cleopatra* with a huge raised, raked stage. Our sound director Henry Bird actually won an American EMMY for his effort. Supposedly because of scheduling, Henry was not allowed to go to the United States to collect his award. Recently, he told me he thought it was 'just' a political award. I admonished him not to do himself down. It was tricky show for sound and Henry did it to perfection. Years later, Editor, John Hawkins won an EMMY for the Liza Minelli Muppet Show. His head of department considered it such an achievement that he insisted John go to Los Angeles to collect it.

The *Julie Andrews Christmas Show 1973* starring Peter Ustinov as Father Christmas, taking Julie back to days of yore. A really nice show. It would feature a sixty piece orchestra with arrangements by Andre Previn. For this show, Julie's new musical director was Ian Fraser, replacing the famed Nelson Riddle.
Born in Hove, Sussex, Ian had performed with the Royal Artillery Band as a harpist, solo concert pianist and percussionist. He was musical director on Anthony Newley's West End hit; *Stop the world, I want to get off.* When it transferred to Broadway he followed and stayed in the USA. Nominated for an Emmy 32 times he won eleven. Ian had perfect pitch, a rare talent. Once, Anthony Newly had a dinner party where a guest accidently clinked a glass. Someone guessed at musical note; 'D'"

Another guest said "G".
Newly rang Ian Fraser in the States;
'Ian?'
'Yeah'
'Ian, what's this?'
Newly tapped the glass.
'*D minor*' said Ian.
'Thanks'

'No problem' said Ian as he hung up.

Now, he was to be Julie Andrew's new musical director. Before starting the production, all the crew heads were treated to a night at the Albert Hall, where, among others, Julie would perform all the Christmas songs destined for the show.

Later, Ian took the dozen, or so, of us to a nearby Chinese (or was it Thai?) restaurant for a slap-up dinner. Nelson Riddle, with his wheelchair bound wife, was in the same restaurant and came over to our table introducing himself to everybody. I was always a great Nelson Riddle fan, his Sinatra arrangements for many albums were renowned. Nelson wished us all good luck for the forthcoming series before departing. Later, when Ian called for bill, the waiter said it had been taken care of by Mr Riddle. Wow! You don't get many Nelson Riddles' to the pound. How he got away by not being called 'Jimmy' I shall never know.

With a sixty piece orchestra playing those Previn arrangements this was going to be something special. Julie is the consummate performer. The opening item was accentuated Jon Scofield's visual talent. Later Julie impeccably mimed *Hark the Herald* despite mouthfuls of polystyrene snowflakes. For this item, we used a brand new echo device called *echoplex* which delayed sound to one's specification. It worked well for trumpet and trombone stabs.

You can catch this on YouTube. Later, Julie finds Peggy Lee posing as the Sugar Plum Fairy. The ensuing medley sees them using jewel-encrusted hand microphones. ATV outside broadcast workshops did the jewelling through the good offices of Keith Wilkinson, that same OB sound guy with the hoofbeats.

We finished the show with Peggy Lee singing *Have yourself a merry little Christmas* in an aeroplane set. It was eight minutes to two o'clock in the afternoon, after which she was due at Heathrow for a flight to Europe. No rehearsal was possible. Lighting control told director Jon Scoffield that going beyond two o'clock would not be allowed (unionism again rearing its ugly head!). Jon replied, quietly that if the light were extinguished he would personally kill someone. They weren't and he didn't.

After the wrap, we started the sound re-mix ready for final layback to VTR working through the night for next day's transmission. At well past midnight, the door to our control room opened and Julie appeared with a huge tray of sandwiches and flasks of coffee. You don't get many Julie Andrews' to the pound either.

Owing to internal ITV management squabbles, this beautifully made Special was transmitted in Britain at eleven thirty at night. What a waste.

Another nice JULIE ANDREWS Special starred a not-so-nice Jackie Gleason. There as a big production number around a snooker table where Jackie Gleason sang the 'You've got trouble in River City' number from *The Music Man.* With radio microphones, at that time, being so unreliable, I covered it on two booms using long, tubular Sennheiser microphones. These allowed voice pick-up to be acceptable allowing lots of headroom, but only provided the microphone was looking directly at the source of sound. Instead of being within four feet with a normal boom microphone, you could easily get away with seven or eight feet. Observant viewers will see these same microphones used over televised snooker tournaments.

The extended 'pool' table was covered in long shot most of the time and the hanging light box in the centre often impeded the booms. We did the lengthy item in several segments much to the chagrin of Mr. Gleason. At the end of the show when the cast were taking bows, Gary Smith (off camera) asked Mr. Gleason to kiss Julie. His reply is not printable, but lip readers will have a good idea. The delightful and professional Miss Julie Andrews, as usual, was magnanimous and polite throughout.

GENE KELLY first came to Elstree with the Sandy Duncan Show in the late sixties. Sandy was a talented and vivacious blonde comedienne well known in the States. And a fantastic dancer. Her Special was to be directed by the Hemion/Smith team. Before studio recording takes place, technical staff are required to attend an outside rehearsal session where they see the show performed (in the rough) and are able to assess their later requirements. Excitedly looking forward to seeing one of my Hollywood idols, I looked around the rehearsal room and could only find a rather scruffy, balding old gentleman reading a newspaper in the far corner of the room. Yes, it was Gene Kelly who 'walked' through the rehearsal avidly reading a script and barely moving a muscle.

Two days later, sitting in sound control, I glanced up at my monitor to see a young-looking, handsome, beautifully garbed Gene Kelly walk onto the set. He sang and danced his way through the programme with consummate ease. Make-up and hair department at their very best. Sandy was in such awe of Gene the show glowed with happiness and jollity. Writer/producer Jack Burns wrote the script (more of Jack later). He was the dead-pan writer and producer personified. Sandy had only to look at his sad downcast face before bursting out laughing. Jack had a store of banana jokes and I would think, to this day, whenever she sees a banana she thinks of Jack Burns.

One production number involved several dancers with Gene and Sandy. Taps would be added later and I had arranged for the dancers to be available in the band room to record this session. Gene Kelly advised me how they did this in Hollywood. By just having two dancers and slipping the track slightly meant the taps were more precise than say, ten dancers trying to all keep exactly together. When he came back years later for the Steve & Eydie Gershwin Special, he was pleased to see we were keeping with his 'Hollywood' routine.

For the aficionado;
People often ask why put the taps on later, surely easier to use the sound associated with the picture when filming. Well, it would be if the shot didn't vary consistently. Most dance sequences are shot in many pieces, often dozens. Also with a change of camera angle, the lighting has to be altered and this could take an hour or more.

When the entire sequence is finally edited, the only original sound to be heard is the track, distant foot taps intermingled with shouting, floor noise and air conditioning. Hence, the choreographer (rarely the dancer) who designed the sequence replaces all that naff sound with perfect taps.

Fred Astaire, the ultimate fusspot would insist on sequences being shot in one take without cuts. This allowed live sound pick-up with his own foot taps often being used. Duets with Ginger Rogers would often involve multiple cuts and re-takes so there were times when even Fred's taps weren't actually his own. They say that Ginger Rogers was an angel putting up with Fred's fussiness, often shooting well into the early hours. I read her biography and she hints at this without accusation.

At the height of her fame, JUDY GARLAND recorded a midnight charity show at the London Palladium. I was on the sub-mix position in the Royal Circle. With fifteen minutes to go, Miss Garland had still not arrived. She also had not attended any rehearsal. It was all going to be a bit off-the-cuff for Jack Parnell and his Orchestra.

Apparently, when she finally arrived she was a bundle of nerves and was hesitant to go on. Her walk-on music was played twice before famed Palladium Stage Manager, Jack Matthews, finally had to literally push her on from the wings. She entered to a tumultuous applause and went on to perform what was perhaps one of her finest concerts ever. After the interval she introduced the very young Liza, her daughter. Sitting on the edge of the stage she looked up at her mum admiringly until the final curtain. Sound

Director Dennis Bassinger probably treasures the tape of that show as his 'show-reel' and rightly so.

LIZA MINELLI starred in one of the many Muppet Shows I was fortunate enough to work on, no longer the tall, gangly girl sitting on the edge of the Palladium stage, instead a polished, talented and beautiful young lady.

I very recently watched this show for the first time something like thirty years after it was made. The production number *Cococabana* featuring Liza is, I think, one of the best the Muppets ever produced. Her performance with life-size Muppets is a choreographed gem. On the dub, using a 'Peg' machine, the in-tempo gunshots were my contribution. This show is among my six favourite Muppet Shows. They don't make 'em like this anymore (not even the modern Muppet Shows).

DICK VAN DYKE co-starred in a Julie Andrews Special entitled Julie & Dick in Covent Garden. This offered the history of that famous theatre in word and song. One huge segment was a sequence outside the theatre involving a street market set with over twenty stalls and dozens of boxes filled with fresh vegetables.

Nearby, sacks of other vegetables were to be danced around and used for props for the big production number devised and choreographed by Paddy Stone. This took up the entire floor area of Studio C. We had hardly started the shoot when an industrial dispute closed the site down for five days. The studios were locked up. On return, the brave dancers and principals had to perform for two long shoot days with rotting vegetables. The smell was dreadful, but no turned up noses on the clip called *Step in Time* to be found on YouTube.

Mr. Van Dyke was the perfect guest star always on set first thing, chatting to the crew before performing arduous dance sequences that pinpointed his talents. He and Julie had of course worked together before (a massive understatement). This was a super production.

EDDIE FISHER brought his fiancée Connie Stevens to record his Special, (I think it only went out in the States?) The show was to open with them discovered in separate dressing rooms. A callboy would tap on both doors and they would emerge meeting up in full song along two corridors onto the stage for the opening sequence. Sounds pretty simple, what on earth could go wrong?

To achieve this, the voices would have to be pre-recorded. Both artistes were placed in the band room vocal booth with headphones singing along with the Jack Parnell Band as we laid down tracks. At one point a retake was necessary. Connie whispered to Eddie that his pitch was slightly off. Nobody could hear this apart from those of us in the sound control room. To our astonishment, he rounded on his fiancée saying *'Don't talk to a star like that honey'*.

My tape operator Roy Nilsen (he of the boom operating fame) transferred this to a cassette which he often played years later to the crew on headphones whenever he deemed it appropriate.

However, it wasn't so funny the next day when we came to start recording on the set. Eddie stopped us all in our tracks by telling Floor Manager, Richard Holloway that he never mimes, that he is a 'live' performer.
Apparently he thought the session the day before was just a rehearsal! That lengthy recording session was elbowed and booms were wheeled in to cover live voice pick-up. This involved a massive lighting reset for Johnnie Rook. Boom shadows can only be avoided by clever lighting (and clever boom operating). Director Jon Scoffield took it all quite calmly and we got under way a good two hours late. If Jon had a cat, I imagined it would, by now, be black and blue.

Eddie could often appear to be a morose character. Once, in the sound control room after listening to a pre-recorded band track his manager was talking heatedly on the phone – during this Eddie asked me for a cigarette. I obliged. Standing behind the desk in my line of sight, he leant across to me and quietly confided

'*Everybody hates me*'.

'*Surely not!*' I retorted, rather embarrassed to say the least.

He whispered a reply '*I even hate myself*'.

Brave Lionel Blair stood in for both artistes throughout the rehearsed dance items because Miss Stevens was often too tired being several months pregnant and Eddie was often 'resting'. Connie had pre-recorded one song and on hearing the result during a camera rehearsal she wanted to re-do her voice track even when the floor was waiting to shoot.

A half-hour tea-break was called and she was ushered into a different studio to re-record her voice track. On returning to the floor, we played the new track for the rehearsal to continue when she announced she still wasn't happy and wanted to do the voice track again. The American producer asked the floor manager to give her his headphones. Only those on production talkback could hear what he said. In quietly modulated tones he made it clear to her that she had two options, go with what we've got - or go home. Actually, I'd rather not say what he did actually tell her but it involved her, as yet, unborn child, an aeroplane ticket and her goddam fiancé. All this quietly interspersed with naughty language.

The finished product gave no indication of the trials experienced during this arduous shoot. In the finale of the Concert Spot before an adoring audience, Eddie gave a thunderous version of '*The Impossible Dream*' that virtually bought the house down. Like all the big stars, on the night, he did it right. I don't remember this show ever being transmitted in Britain.

RICHARD WIDMARK with those ice blue eyes is someone I shall never forget. He was recording a television drama at Elstree and rushing through reception, I accidentally crashed into him as he was leaving the elevator. I spluttered an apology as he stared at me without a word.

Two hours later, leaving the canteen, I turned to talk to someone before quickly turning again to crash into Richard Widmark. If those ice blue eyes had been death rays, I wouldn't be here now.

In 1972 the seven episodes of THE STRAUSS FAMILY were made. We recorded all the music at the ATV studios with MD Cyril Ornadel. Cyril was adamant that everything should be final mixed before he left the site. Apparently, he had suffered in the past from mix-downs without his presence.

These recordings culminated in the huge orchestral rendition of *The Blue Danube*. Used ultimately in the final shot in episode seven of Johann Strauss (the younger) on his deathbed. The strings of *The Blue Danube* swelled as the camera pulled out for the wide shot, his body surrounded by hundreds of flowers. It was both poignant and heart rending.

Another great moment, when he orchestra was playing without the maestro in the Sperl Ballroom. Suddenly, the doctor approaches the bandstand with solemn gait. The orchestra, sensing what was coming, stopped playing instrument by instrument. Difficult for them to mime as it had been pre-recorded. The maestro was dead. The deathbed sequence showed Johann surrounded by hundreds of flowers.
This was a Cecil Clarke production with David Reid and David Giles directing. I was allowed to be alongside John Hawkins at the edit. When we got to one of the many sequences, where drama was interspersed with music, I was able to balance the two in the edit. This was a rare occasion. Sound oiks were rarely allowed inside the hallowed halls of the editing suites.

The cast was stupendous. Anne Stallybrass; Derek Jacobi; Jane Seymour; Georgina Hale; Michael Bryant; David de Keyser; Geoffrey Segal and Margaret Whiting in the principal roles. Try booking that lot today. Eric Woolfe and Stuart Wilson played the elder and younger Strauss's. Importantly, they both learned the art of conducting to extraordinary lengths.

Two huge ballroom sets were constructed for the musical sequences in Studio C. Some eighty pieces of music of varying size orchestras were recorded on the original session and as explained all mixed down at the time. Regretfully, Cyril had not taken into account that one ballroom was an outside venue. I had mixed down all of the big orchestra tracks with echo and this did not suit the exterior Sperl Ballroom where a dryer sound would have worked better.

David Reid devised sequences where dance hall scenes would suddenly cut to Strauss household dramatic scenes with the music still running before returning in triumph to the ballroom. The mixture of the tumultuous family drama alternating with happy, gay ballroom sequences could not have worked better.

It is not generally known that Johann Strauss the Younger was the Michael Jackson of his day. When he visited New York, a group of over a thousand musicians in Central Park were assembled in tribute to play his *'Blue Danube'*. The gathering was so immense that a cannon had to be fired so the musicians could start in unison! The entire STRAUSS FAMILY series is available in a DVD boxed set from Acorn Media UK.

THE MELODY DANCES was a dance band show coming from a south London ballroom, transmitted live 11.20 at night. Cyril Stapleton's band accompanied guest singers and they even included a *'Come Dancing'* segment. Cyril later worked with Max Bygraves on his *'Singalong with Max'* series. This was another happy show to work on. The lovely Kaye Sisters were regulars. Any show that requires the audience to join in and sing along usually provides a sound problem. The orchestra and the stage have to be fed to the audience at such a level that it doesn't colour their contribution. The term colour describes an event where an unwanted sound affects the wanted sound. i.e., the audience singing cannot be marred by a loud orchestra which will be inadvertently heard through the audience microphones. Cyril understood this and dropped the orchestra front line just keeping with a quiet rhythm section. Sounds basic, but a lot of musical directors were reluctant to degrade their arrangements.

The DES O'CONNOR Shows went well as a summer replacement in the States sponsored by Kraft and called The Kraft Music Hall. It even extended to a second series. Whether this was due to the American executive producer Mort Lachman's desire for another season of golf at Carnoustie, is a matter of conjecture. (Mort Lachman, died in Hollywood on his ninety first birthday nineteenth of March 2009).

Des had all the advantages of big time guest stars of the Jack Benny calibre and the '*I say, I say*' segment with the likes of Roger Moore, Raquel Welch, Norman Wisdom and visiting superstars popping in to do a gag, certainly enhancing the show. A Kraft representative ensured (thankfully) that no 'cheesy' jokes crept into the script. I understand a compilation of these American shows is available on DVD (October 2009).

Des had an easy-going vocal style but, as I previously explained, if he couldn't hear his voice coming back from the PA, he was unhappy (even doomed). I gave him PA of his voice belting out of a series of loud speakers dotted around the studio, under the audience area and behind the cyclorama. He was more than happy with that, although other sound directors throughout the industry may have considered I went too far. They were probably being pressed for a similar rig. Keep the talent happy!

Producer, Mort Lachman was a Hollywood legend. He produced Bob Hope throughout his career. Mort attended all the dubbing sessions' often not appearing to pay attention. Peter Wernham, the head of post-production sound, was mixing one Des O'Connor show with me alongside. Mort had nodded off and we got to a particularly tricky bit of the show where sound had to be dipped, raised and dipped again at precise times. I can't go in to the whys and wherefores. Peter did a couple of takes, neither worked too well. Finally he got one take that was . . . pretty good. He whispered to me;

'Did that work?'

'Not bad at all' I quietly replied.

Suddenly, Mort, with eyes still closed, spoke;

'Mort didn't like it'.

Other American producers came to ATV and many of those shows were never transmitted in Britain. Most of the American output were produced by the Smith/Hemion team, they include;

The Kopykats Series (stolen by ITV to become *Who Do You Do*) starred Frank Gorshin and Rich Little. Probably two of the finest impressionists ever.

The Herb Alpert Specials.

Burt Bacharach Specials

Barbra Streisand & other musical instruments.

Peter Pan with Danny Kaye and Mia Farrow (the first stereo production to come out of Elstree for American transmission using radio channels. 1974).

Ann-Margret Olsen Special and the Ann-Margret Smith Special.

Bing Crosby Merrie Olde Christmas Special with David Bowie.

Sammy Davis Special.

Julie on Sesame Street

Julie Andrews & Jackie Gleason Special.

Julie and Dick (Van Dyke) in Covent Garden.

Julie's Favourite Things with Peter Sellers.

Julie's Christmas Show with Peter Ustinov and Peggy Lee.

Steve Lawrence and Eydie Gorme - Gershwin and Cole Porter Specials.

Gary Smith and Dwight Hemion were also involved in an advisory capacity with the first, and most important series (1976) of THE MUPPET SHOW.

Hemion and Smith were not always at Elstree, they had other fish to fry in the States flitting back and forth.

***

10. Peter Pan – the 1974 version.

J.M. BARRIE'S CLASSIC TALE Peter Pan had been a regular Christmas Special diet in the United States. Starring Mary Martin and originally made in the 1950s the production was considered good enough to continually repeat year after year. Gary and Dwight decided to break with tradition and update the show sponsored by *Hallmark Cards.* It would star Mia Farrow as Peter Pan, Danny Kaye as Mr. Darling and Captain Hook, Paula Kelly at Tiger Lily, Virginia McKenna as Mrs. Darling and Briony McRoberts as Wendy. John Gielgud would narrate the two-hour production. Anthony Newley and Leslie Bricusse would write an original composition of songs. Ian Fraser would be musical director while the choreography would be in the capable hands of Oscar winner Michael Kidd (*Seven Brides for Seven Brothers*) and many other films.

A challenge for me was that for the first time ever, we would be involved in a stereo production. The first task was to record the music. This entailed a large orchestra recorded onto multi-track with sufficient tracks left blank to add artistes' voices later. The arrangements, by Dave Lindup and Peter Knight were top class. Before shooting began, artists would be called in to add their voice tracks. They were then re-recorded onto cassette for the artistes to take home and learn for later miming.

Danny Kaye was one of the last to arrive. Apparently he came straight from his hotel after flying in. It was a quiet Saturday afternoon and he was due at around 5:00 pm in the Studio C band room and being the big star would always be accompanied by production staff.

To our surprise, he arrived at 2:00 pm and security had guided him to the bandroom where, startled by being the only people to greet him, he quietly opening his script and started to read his lyrics in advance. Later, we arranged to play the band tracks for him to listen to before going for a voice recording.

Danny Kaye seemed a quiet, almost studious man and Roger Banks, my sound technician in the band room, ensured that he was happy with his headphone playback level, microphone position, stool and music stand height, etc. An eager Roger Banks offered refreshments which Mr Kaye politely refused. In sound control we had two TV monitors looking at the band room. One long shot and one close on Danny. This often enabled us to foresee a problem or a request before the event.

I kept a close eye on things because our Roger could be described as a bit of a loose cannon. I had previously advised him to keep shtum but, during a pause, Roger decided to talk to Danny. He related how many fans in the sound department were looking forward to seeing him. How one sound guy, Freddie Abbott, actually knew all the lyrics of Danny's songs by heart. Danny listened to Roger politely and in his enthusiasm, Roger even ventured to relay the lyrics of one particular item concerning *"The Vessel with the Pestle"* (from the film *The Court Jester*). After several bad attempts Danny quietly exploded;

'If you must sing my songs get them right! It goes like this…..'

He then proceeded to sing the lyric all through at breakneck speed. Roger looked on in admiration and at the end remarked; *'that's the one.'*

Danny took a strange liking to Roger calling him 'Stringbean' for the rest of the entire production. Roger was tall and thin and many times during the shoot, Danny would yell out *'Stringbean'* requesting coffee or a peek at the script.

All voice-recordings were completed on time except for Mia Farrow. Ian Fraser was concerned that Mia would have a problem, as some of the songs were quite tricky to sing and Mia was not a singer. Eventually we had a late night session with Mia in the band room vocal booth, and Ian upstairs with us in sound control. The most difficult song for her would be a ballad called *A Song Called Love*. This was a pivotal song describing the loneliness of Peter Pan and the unattainable dream constantly haunting him. Ian figured if she could get this song in the can, the others would be easy. Several attempts in the vocal booth were unsuccessful and Mia was getting despondent. At one point she even questioned whether she was right for this role.

Much later, Ian had the idea of bringing her up to the comfort of our control room out of the daunting ambience of the lonely band room. He then sent Stringbean out to get a Chinese meal and a couple of bottles of wine. Boreham Wood High Street had several outlets open even at this late hour. A microphone and cans were set up in the adjacent production control room where we had visual contact via darkened glass. By midnight, after a convivial 'supper' we had four very acceptable takes on tape.

Mia, sting alongside at the sound desk, was thrilled to see how we could mix between takes and come up with a definitive version. The rest of the songs were successfully recorded that night. Here's the song itself, check out Mia's perfect miming. This was a take one sequence.

http://www.youtube.com/watch?v=IkYy6MsAa_w

Shooting began with the flying sequences. Studio B contained Wendy's bedroom. Kirby Wires were used in this set. Mia was flown into Wendy's room ostensibly looking for her shadow (song: *"I'm better with you than without")*. Kirby Wires are notoriously difficult to come to terms with and Mia crashed into the bedroom wall more than once, but always with a rueful smile and a joke before another take.

Danny Kaye, resplendent in his Captain Hook outfit, spent some of his break times and scene change periods in sound control, regaling us with stories of his career (greatly encouraged by us). How Basil Rathbone had not sufficiently rehearsed his sword fighting scenes in the iconic film *The Court Jester.* Apparently, a sword swirling double was often used, much to Danny's disgust.

He spoke of his nervousness during the making of his first ever movie *Up In Arms* and his admiration for Sylvia Fine (his wife) who guided him throughout his early career. He complained bitterly about the lack of time to learn lyrics on this production. In 'the old days' he would be given weeks, not days! However, during shooting, his miming of his tracks was impeccable.

One sequence was *'The Rock'* – a lonely, fog swirling set nicely lit by Johnnie Rook. In this sequence, Captain Hook and Peter Pan nearly confront each other. Here, Danny would perform the song *'By Hook Or By Crook'* a showpiece with fast talking lyrics that utilised his skills of miming to perfection before being chased by the dreaded crocodile.

Hook and Pan are alone, warily looking for each other. The camera sees them both but they do not see each other. This was a tricky bit of choreography by Michael Kidd, sometimes stretching the imagination if not performed to perfection. Danny was visibly unhappy with the choreography and things in general. Gary Smith, always on the floor with the artistes, tried to console him whilst Mia stood by keeping shtum.

Eventually, the camera crew were stood down then sent home. The track was replayed many times as

Michael and Danny tried to re-plot choreography. Finally, seemingly exasperated, Danny left the set. An hour later, floor manager Richard Holloway ascertained that he had left the site. Early wrap for all.

The next day, to everybody's amazement, he had not only left the site but also left Great Britain to return home to Los Angeles to ruminate. There was a minor union strike on also at this time so the intriguing 'rock in the fog' set went dark.

When Danny eventually returned, the producer Gary Smith and director Dwight Hemion invited him to *Lorenzo's*, a top London restaurant to lighten the atmosphere. Danny rejected the offer saying he was jet-lagged and too tired.

Gary and Dwight's party went to the restaurant and after a superb meal the chef emerged from the kitchen to enquire whether the food was to their satisfaction. It was Danny Kaye, resplendent in a chef's outfit. Being a renowned superb cook, Danny had arranged with the restaurant to supervise the meals for the Hemion/Smith table.

The *'Rock in the fog'* sequence was finally completed to everybody satisfaction. Captain Hook departs leaving Peter Pan to stand atop the rock in swirling mist to declare the famous line;

'To die would be an awfully great adventure'.

In the following week, the rest of the show went swimmingly. The sword fight sequences with Peter Pan aboard the pirate ship, involving Danny singing and generally leaping about, were quite arduous. A stunt double was employed for some of the more athletic moves. This was not a great idea. The double was forty years younger, slim and very athletic. It didn't gel.

After completion, brilliant musical director Ian Fraser returned to the States with a video rough cut to compose the musical underscore with frame accuracy. On returning, Ian conducted the Jack Parnell Orchestra while we recorded more than an hour's underscore to picture. Unusually, I mixed this underscore while listening to the dialogue track at normal level. This way, we ensured that no dialogue was obscured by music. How often this happens today in drama and documentaries! Also, by mixing music at low level certain sections of the orchestra could be enhanced. Normally, a full volume mix played later at a much quieter level was not always faithful to the concept.

The finished product was something we were all proud of. The beautiful set designs by David Chandler included an underground Peter Pan hideout beneath a tree in the Neverland sequences. Johnny Rook lit with his usual flair whilst Bill Brown's camera crew gave it all a super look. Later, the entire crew gathered in the band room for a playback of the first ever stereo production to come out of Elstree. The show went out in the States with the option for viewers to tune in to their local radio stations to hear the stereo mix while watching their mono televisions. Apparently, this was great success. This was 1975, long before television transmission could handle stereo sound.

Regretfully, after just a two-year run, the networks reverted to the Mary Martin version. *What the hay . . .* that's Show Business!

There are clips on YouTube where Gary expounds theories on American versus British television production. He mentions ATV Elstree at great length and with much affection.

A nicer pair of multi-talented guys you would be hard to find. They had a control room party trick where Dwight would ask the vision mixer to write down the name of a playing card. Then he would ask Gary (on the studio floor) to tell us what the vision mixer had written. Gary would reply in about ten words that he was too busy to mess about. Then he would pause and say . . . ten of diamonds (or whatever). We never did discover the hidden code of those ten words.

***

11. No Excuses to Jimi Hendrix.

IN 1982 WE EMBARKED on; 'No Excuses'. A re-titling of Barrie Keefe's tale 'Bastard Angels' about a fading rock star, Shelley Maze played by Charlotte Cornwell. An established actress, Charlotte had quite a rock-ish voice and the fourteen songs for the eight one-hour episodes were performed either in the studio or on location in rock venues. The songs were all written by a brilliant keyboard player Andy J. Clark leading the heavy rock band.

For the series opening sequence, Shelley arrives by Rolls Royce to inspect the baronial hall she has purchased. The Rolls going up the drive took a minute or so, and on the sound dub, I played a single low note increasing the level gradually until it hit a crescendo as she slammed the car door when we crashed into the huge opening number. It was a dramatic moment par excellence!

The series was a costly production, no expense spared. The floors of the awe-inspiring mansion sets were entirely covered with flagstones (tricky for tracking cameras). The dialogue content was often daring and very dramatic and harrowing; Charlotte showed a huge depth of acting talent. Not a singer by any means, but her performance as the gritty, slightly over the hill, rock star, Shelley Maze, was, to my mind, very convincing.

We did the show in stereo. Roy Battersby, a well-known drama director, appeared not to care one way or the other until I asked him to come in to the sound control room and listen to the rehearsal of Alfred Burke playing Shelley's butler.

The scene was a huge thirty foot wooden table in the baronial hall. Alfred Burke was laying the table for something like thirty guests with silver and expensive glasses and crockery. The sound of his footsteps walking round the table on flagstones and rattling cutlery was really effective in stereo. Especially with a little echo added!

Roy was enthralled and from that moment on he thought in terms of stereo. Boom operating skills were changed for stereo. You no longer followed the artiste around, you kept the stereo microphone still in the centre of shot so that natural left and right noises remained left and right to match the picture being taken.

We visited a couple of London clubs, *The Fridge* in Brixton comes to mind, a lively venue where we recorded our *No Excuses* rock group with Charlotte singing live with a real, unsuspecting, audience. Later, a German outdoor concert was faked in studio C. The deafening levels from our rock band was such that some of the crew were unable to stay in the vicinity – *'it shook my rib cage'* one cameraman complained.

To try and emulate what this would sound like at home, we discarded the usual sound dubbing suite loudspeakers (some £1500 each) and mixed the entire show on a domestic stereo television set in an effort to simulate home viewing. Having acquired tinnitus in both ears after years of too loud monitoring, I advise budding dubbing mixers to try this method.

Titled ENCORE, an eighth programme of NO EXCUSES was put together consisting of just the musical items. Later, an album was produced of the recorded music from our show by CBS records which we re-mixed at the Manfred Mann Studios in south London. I arrived at this studio on the first morning to find it deserted. Around three o'clock the musicians would drift in, usually half asleep. After bacon sandwiches (and some liquid refreshment!) at tea-time, they finally got ready to start listening to the already record tracks to add 'finishing touches'. Approaching midnight, they all seem to come alive, just as I was dozing off.

I don't think the programme got a good transmission slot. It was also critically panned as well. The casting was criticized up front. I believe that some thought an established singer like Kikki Dee was more suited to the role. But the dramatic segments of the show demanded an experienced actress and, to my mind, Charlotte filled that role admirably.

Do you cast a singer that has to do some serious acting or an actor who has to do some serious singing? Whatever, it was such a good story that a re-make today would, I think, be a great success.

Yes, the band in *No Excuses* was loud but not as loud as a show that I was given the chance to mix before becoming a sound director in the early sixties. This was a children's programme, hosted by Pete Murray and going out live at 5.30 pm. The guest band turned out to be none other than Jimi Hendrix.

His guitar were so loud I had to put huge screens around the drums to avoid the drums being swamped. Normally, one would screen drums to avoid leaking into other band microphones. I had also increased the number of drum mics from two to eight, cutting the level required from each to a minimum, therefore assisting the screening out of Jimi's guitar.

Cameras had to operate way back from the set on different lenses as the excessive sound level caused microphony, a condition that affected the picture causing it to 'wobble' It was reported that during transmission in Studio A, Jimi Hendrix could be heard in the canteen some hundred yards away leaking through 'sound-proof' doors. Pads were installed into the microphone chain to stop overloading and distortion. Today, digital everything has solved the microphony problem.

After a rehearsal in the morning, Jimi would come up to sound control and listen to a playback. He appeared to be a sad individual; often so morose he was unable to communicate. I'm sure he wasn't always like this, but for me, having only been promoted to a number two a couple of months ago it was difficult to get him to guide me on his group sound.
This was my opportunity to shine should a future sound director opening occur it was quite an important session and I really felt for the guy, obviously something was amiss. I was given this programme as a trial by the Head of Sound, Des Gray. Jimi Hendrix probably wasn't considered all that big deal at that stage. Had he been as huge as he became, I would never have got that chance. I like to think my promotion to Sound Director some weeks later had something to do with the brilliant Mr. Hendrix and his extraordinary talent (and sound level!). I wish I had a video of that programme – on second thoughts, best left to the memory!

The sound director's board was held a week, of so, later. Sitting opposite the hot seat would be the head of sound, a senior sound director and possibly someone from engineering (the one to fear, question-wise). I got through my interview quite well considering my past experiences in this realm. The practical questions like microphone placement I could cope with. The technical ones not quite so cocky. I hypothesised that bass drum microphone placement should be tried on both sides of the bass drum. Vibraphone mic placement should also be tried *below* the instrument as a better pick-up might often be achieved. Experimentation was the keynote. Bearing in mind that not all bass drums, or vibraphones were the same. This went down quite well.

Then came the engineering wallah;

'What are the advantages of a trap valve before the final chain as opposed to after? – How does a trap valve work?'

Another couple of tricky ones followed. I batted these away saying I knew *how* to operate these pieces of equipment but I didn't actually know how they were constructed. My job was to get the best out of them and if they failed, called someone who could solve it without too much loss of time. My Jimi Hendrix thing came up and I finished up about 50/50. What I lost on the roundabouts I gained on the swings.

Two days later, I got the letter. Successful candidate etc, etc. starting immediately at £2040 pa. Des Gray, the head of sound, came out to my house and advised me not to come into work for three days as my appointment had caused a bit of resentment among the department. I had only been a number two for four months, some guys had served years waiting for promotion.

The long and short, I got sent to Coventry for quite a period. I had taken over crew four and gradually gained their backing by doing a couple of good jobs and getting asked to do bigger and better productions. So, they gained as well.

In retrospect, as far as my interview went, my Radio Luxembourg experience trumped all.

***

12. Some more (boring?) sound stuff.

I HAVE ALWAYS BEEN a keen advocate of the close mike technique when recording bands and groups. Even the superb BBC Proms output uses booster microphones dotted through the huge Albert Hall stage, they aren't used all the time, perhaps, but available to goose up a French horn, or a harp gliss. I know that music was written before microphones were invented, everything was virtually self-balancing, but now, cameras sneak in for a crafty close-up of an oboe solo, or whatever – the booster microphones are vital.

Close microphones on drums are a prime example. I liked my mikes almost touching the skins and cymbals. Many rock roadies seem to think two microphones high above the drummer work well in 'opening' the drum sound. But fading those up, to my mind, negates the quality of an up-front, driving drum sound. Generally speaking, the closer the microphone, the less level required hence less unobtrusive pickup.

This doesn't necessarily apply to opera singers who have massive voices. The nineties *'Three Tenors'* concert programme always baffled me, two microphones on each one, with giant black windshields and inches from their chins?

Not many will get the opportunity of recording a big band these days; you don't always need masses of microphones. As explained, for radio, we only used ten on the Ted Heath band. If the band is in shot, a different set-up is required. Those five saxophones would need five microphones.

In the recording studio, a saxophone section will almost certainly be doubling, clarinets or flutes etc. At Elstree, like other recording studios, we had separate microphones available for this, meaning a normal saxophone section (5) could have ten, or more, microphones at their disposal.

Often band layouts were played with by the designer wanting a pretty look. I recollect doing a Tom Jones series with director Phillip Casson. The designer had put the band in little boxes, rather like the Celebrity Squares set. He obviously thought it looked pretty but the musicians found it difficult hearing everybody else – result, we had to pre-record the orchestra which then involved miming. Not a happy outcome.

A dance band has to be set out a certain way, both visually and sound-wise. Later, the Tom Jones Concert Spot with the Jack Parnell band fronted by Johnnie Spence proved to be a virtually perfect combination.

> For the ultimate band sound, may I recommend?
> THE ROAD SHOW
> With Stan Kenton and his orchestra, June Christy and the Four Freshman.
> (Capitol Records Inc).

This fantastic album recorded at Purdue University in Layayette, Indiana is, to my mind, the epitome of sound balancing at its best with the finest modern jazz orchestra in the world . . . bar none! - In *'My Old Flame'* the five trumpet players perform a perfect combination trill that can never be bettered.

Recorded over two nights by Capitol Record engineers it brings goose-bumps to me, even talking about it. Five trumpets. Five trombones. Five saxophones and a rhythm section enhanced by Cuban drums, all recorded under perfect acoustical conditions.

You will never hear a finer big band sound than this. It was recorded in 1959 while I was still at Radio Luxembourg fiddling about with shows like Primo Scala's Accordion band.

Ah well, back to the script.

Acoustic guitars are notoriously difficult to record. Finger noises are often annoying - try experimenting with different mics and distances. I once placed a glass screen in front of a solo guitar player aiming the microphone at that screen. It lessened the finger noise considerably. Then again, some classical guitar recordings seem to especially feature the 'finger noise' – you pay your money, take your choice. That's sound balancing for you.

In the ATV band room at Elstree, picking up the string section was always a problem. Despite screening, the drums and brass would usually infiltrate. Often we would put the strings on afterwards, although this would presented a union problem. For instance, if you wanted a second take of the strings, they often assumed you would add that to the first take, giving the effect of a larger string section, less work for the guys.

A musician's union spy sometimes visited the control room to oversee sessions of that nature. Of course, if the 'spy' didn't have technical knowledge to know whether take one had actually been erased, it was 'highly possible' that both takes were sometimes used (ahem!).

These days many string sections use individual microphone pick-ups attached to the instrument. I used these in a night club-type series in Norway on an eight piece string section (more about that later). It was some years ago and early days for pick-ups. Most violinists treasure their instrument like a gout sufferer protecting his foot from passers-by and even when our Norwegian string group allowed usage they were very difficult to sound balance.

I'm sure those problems have now been eradicated, certainly after seeing and hearing some orchestras, I sit there in wonderment at the quality of the string section pick-up. Recently, the marvellous BBC Electric Proms broadcast a Burt Bacharach concert with a big swinging band and a huge string section, all on pick-ups. Super show, super sound, couldn't have got that in 'the old days'.

SKY ARTS recently transmitted a super Diana Krall night club performance from Rio de Janeiro. Her four piece rhythm group is backed by a local Brazilian orchestra who were miked up in the old conventional fashion, lots of microphones above lots of stings, brass and woodwind. I would have loved to have had my hands on that sound desk. The mix was beautiful. If SKY ARTS re-show it, be sure to catch it.

The ultimate good string sound is, of course, a large number of strings with slung microphones above them; i.e., the BBC Proms. Thank God for the BBC. Would any other broadcaster spend the time, money and effort to bring such joy to our eyes and ears via the beautifully acoustically treated Royal Albert Hall venue?

There are so many ways to record orchestras. I have an innovative Harry James record that was made in the fifties where the band self-balanced around one microphone in the studio, while the output went directly to a cutting styli onto a 10" acetate master record. Four tracks were played consecutively filling one side of the record. I can only conclude that Harry was a bit of a pioneer and wanted to test the theory. It wasn't at all bad, Harry - quite a successful experiment (especially bearing in mind he probably had Betty Grable constantly on his mind at that time).

Musical instruments played by marvellous musicians have always been a fascination for me. Oh to be able to whip up and down a violin like many do, or play a piano concerto totally from memory? I've had to content myself with listening and enjoying.

***

13. Up a bit . . . fire - the diversity of ATV.

ANOTHER INTERESTING FACET OF THE early days at ATV was the advertising magazines. A crafty way to increase the revenue beyond the constraints of commercial breaks, the ad-mag was usually a fifteen minute programme in a shop or a pub In ITV's Jim's Inn, the hosts would replicate village life in a pub before extolling the virtues of goods to be mysterious discovered on the pub counter.

ATV's contribution to the genre was a show featuring comedians John Campbell and John Singer. One of the products was a home-made beer, I'm pretty sure it was Davenports? They would talk the product at length before swigging a whole half pint down in one go while we played a jingle, about eight seconds, I believe?

Sound director Peter Hubbard gave me the chance to mix one show. It was good training ground. Peter took over the gram operating chair. The ad-mag was only intended for the Birmingham area thus we were unable to view transmission output from our Elstree studios.

We were nearly halfway through the show when Birmingham transmission control got on the line to say we would be on air in five minutes and why were we still rehearsing? Panic stations - we had been given a bum timing and the floor hastily worked hard to go back to the beginning of the show, rearranging the pack shots etc. Director Fred Wilby, more used to kid's talent shows, hadn't quite grasped the severity of the problem. When he did, he found it all too much and left the control room.

When we eventually re-started, the PA, Mary Selway and vision mixer Moyra Bird took over, Mary calling the shots and Moyra cutting the pictures as if nothing untoward had happened. When we got to the home-beer segment and the two John's had to gulp down another glass of beer in one go – they couldn't. Beer stained shirts prevailed. Incidentally, Mary Selway later left England to become a hot-shot casting director in Hollywood.

WEST END TALES was a nice comedy cops & conmen caper directed by Jimmy Gatward. Jimmy was a film director; he lured me to leave the comfort of my luxurious control room and operate on the studio floor with a floor mixer and headphones; . . . oh and a take bell, an unknown item in television broadcasting.

This experience whetted my appetite for the film industry quite a bit. Jimmy found out I was from Leytonstone, in east London.

'*So was I*' he responded '.

'*And so was Alfred Hitchcock*' I added.

He further enquired what road I lived in. I told him; '*what number?*

"*288*' I replied.

'*Ah* . . . 'he shot back '*I lived at number 144*'.

Jimmy had a marvellous system of working, shooting the master shot of the whole scene in one take. Then single shots followed by two/three shots from both angles, then the master shot once more. It may seem convoluted but in edit he'd have everything covered to perfection. I began to think, if this efficiency happens in films, what am I doing here in telly?

Later, we did a lot of location work in the West End, always at weekends when it would be quiet. Oh yeah! 6 am is when road works start in the West End with shop alarm bells ringing unattended for hours on end. On one occasion we had to change the shoot venue three times being unable to contact shop owners with blaring alarm bells ringing. Living round that neighbourhood couldn't have been much fun. This situation is now even worse. The City on a Saturday morning (2018) is crammed packed tight with cranes, digging and generators. Far worse than those alarms going off that we experienced.

On West End Tales it was always freezing cold and Roger Wilkinson (my number two) and I looked forward to a lunchtime hot toddy before the afternoon shoot. Jimmy Gatward was not happy about the crew boozing (quite rightly too!) and he instructed Richard Holloway the first assistant director to collect names of the dreadful imbibers. I believe Richard lost the list later that day.

Once the pub was attended by Tony Hawes and his wife, who lived in that neck of the woods. (More about Tony later). They had been shopping and parked three carrier bags by the bar counter to have a chat with the crew who were known to them. Even Jimmy Gatward joined in with a large orange juice. After an hour and both Tony and his wife (and the contents of those bags) were looking very bedraggled.

It was that cold . . . . I used the cans as ear muffs.

Jimmy decided to post produce after the entire series was shot. Part way through dubbing, he unexpectedly (to say the least) won the franchise to run the new Southern Television Company, now to be called TVS. Jimmy shot up in the world to chauffeured cars and high tech meetings. He left West End Tales to us. The show was not un-like MINDER, very light and very enjoyable. I think Mr. Gatward went to Australia to get back into films after TVS.

A touch of technicality; On West End Tales we used the filmic Nagra tape machine to record all sound for eventual relaying onto master video tape after final edit. This would ensure the sound only suffered two or three generations.

It may be worth explaining this procedure at the post production stage. The quad video tape allowed just two outer tracks for sound storage. These tracks were far from hi-fi and after editing from master to master then copying and recopying by other transmission stations, often ended up sixth or more generation sound. Magnetic tape was not generation friendly and with the consequent increase in background noise the finished sound product did not fare well. By relaying, the sound from the Nagra onto the final edited videotape, the sound would be much more acceptable.

The importance of this will be obvious in the BOB HOPE ROYAL GALA segment (see The Freelance Life) where, because the sound multi-track tapes were lost, the sound went out in the States something like 9th generation. Today, of course, with digital sound reproduction, a hundred transfers from one source to another would not affect sound reproduction one iota.

Bob Monkhouse, that consummate professional comedian, was involved in many ATV productions. I had the pleasure of working with him at Radio Luxembourg. He was a constant visitor to Hertford Street with his partner Dennis Goodwin to record a series of record programmes entitled 'You're The Tops'. Bob had an incredible memory for names and gags. He always knew everybody's name at the Hertford Street studios, even after months of absence. Dennis Goodwin was a little hazier. He once went out to buy cigarettes having been directed to nearby Shepherds Market. He never returned that afternoon

Given any subject; Bob, just like Tommy Trinder, would immediately have three gags to suit that subject. They had card-indexed memories able to ad-lib seemingly for hours. Bob appeared at St. Albans Town Hall, some years ago where a heavy fall of snow had attracted only a handful of theatregoers. Bob sat on the edge of the stage, got the handful present to move to the front row seats and said;

'I've left more people at home than this'.

A local paper critic wrote; if you weren't there, you missed a classic performance from Mr. Monkhouse. I believe that.

At ATV, Bob Monkhouse hosted many game shows including Celebrity Squares, Family Fortunes, and memorably, the Golden Shot. This was a live Sunday afternoon programme where the middle segment was a pop group. The group would arrive early Sunday morning, having invariably travelled overnight from a gig. They would either play live or pre-record a track after a hasty rig, but voices were almost invariably live.

Unionism prevented us from using their hit record sound, which invariably took days, if not weeks to produce. On the whole, we tried to emulate their latest hit, but generally we were on a loser. It wasn't beyond the realms of possibility that the musicians or singers on the record weren't the same guys that turned up for the Golden Shot gig.

Apart from this sound commitment, the Golden Shot was a cacophony of sound problems, from audience pick-up to a series of multi-microphones, bells ringing, spot effects and the dreaded telephone line sequence where a viewer would finally instruct Bernie the Bolt - *'Up a bit – left a bit - right a bit . . . . . fire'*

Sometimes, less than a minute before the phone line was needed, I would monitor the line to discover the planned contestant wasn't on the line. Another contestant would be waiting on an alternate line. Bob Monkhouse was never put out by late changes, he could ad lib his way through anything. Out of dozens of Golden Shots, I think I wouldn't be exaggerating to say I only got on third absolutely right.

I remember a contestant complaining that the allotted thirty seconds to fire was cut short. Being a live transmission, the only record of the show was the sound tape we recorded on the day. The next day (Monday morning) I was called in to play this recording to the angry contestant while a production assistant timed the spot he complained about. A dispute arose as to her pressing the stop watch too soon thereby (allegedly) shortening the shoot-the-bolt time. Eventually, I satisfied everybody by cutting the exact segment where he fired the bolt - and laying the tape lengthways on a corridor floor. Measured at 15 inches per second this meant that 30 seconds equalled four hundred and fifty inches in length.

Armed with a brand new tape measure, the now not-so-angry contestant discovered that they not only had he been given the correct time, but six and half inches over! Six and a half inches! I really wish Bob had been there for that performance, he would have made great play of that. I was more than happy with the result having been called in on a notional day off (eight hours at double time).

Apart from The Golden Shot, being live, other shows were multi-recorded, sometimes three or more a day. Bob had a warm-up for the afternoon audiences and another for the evening (slightly risqué). The next night even that warm-up was different. He gauged his warm-ups to the feel of the particular audience.

Bob was an old movies aficionado. He could recite the names of hundreds of lesser-known actors from that period. Apparently, Bob was an amazing collector. Matchboxes, picture postcards and just about anything you can think of. And, of course, his famous joke book collection He was also known to record every channel on his multiple banks of tape recorders. More of Bob later on the American summer replacement show BONKERS.
One thing for sure, there will never be another Bob Monkhouse.

Although ATV was renowned for the quality and quantity of the light entertainment scene, the drama department was responsible for a massive output of top quality programming. Famous names were on call through the talent agencies associated with the company. In association with H.M. Tennant, acting and writing talent for one-off dramas were readily available. All the sets were painted a soft green. Apparently, this worked well for black and white transmissions. We called it Tennant Green!

CLAYHANGER, the Arnold Bennett author of the happenings in the potteries industries in the nineteenth century was a massive project undertaken by the ATV drama department, David Reid produced the epic 1-hour programmes in twenty-six episodes. He and John Davies shared the directing. Douglas Livingstone wrote the scripts from the famous series of books.

The shows starred Janet Suzman; Peter McEnery; Harry Andrews; Dennis Quilley and Denholm Elliott. With dozens of other slightly lesser parts, a massive set budget and studio booking, together with masses of specially written music it is doubtful whether such a project today would be financially viable.

A huge series of back lot sets were constructed depicting the Potteries locations and we went on location to the Potteries on several occasions. Real Colliery Pit Bands were utilized for the 'Five Towns' celebration sequences. My commitment lasted for eighteen episodes, leaving for other musical projects. Sound Director Henry Bird took over the reins for the last eight episodes.

I recently purchased the entire DVD set. The atmosphere surely capture the times nicely? Difficult to isolate a performer for best acting but Harry Andrews would probably come close. My favourites, however, would be Janet Suzman and Peter McEnery.

14. Luxembourg 'more ancient' tid-bits.

AT THE HEIGHT OF David Whitfield's career during the Radio Luxembourg period, we toured with his popular show featuring Ronnie Aldrich and the Squadronaires, the Max Jaffa Strings and Mr. & Mrs. Smith's Five Little Boys. Can't remember who the sponsor was.

David, a former brickie from Hull had a charismatic career. Every time he stepped onto stage, a girlish yell would erupt. Nowadays, these yells are pretty much par for the course, even on quiz programmes but it was heady stuff then. He never appeared to have a nervous bone in his body and his natural microphone technique was superb. Sound-wise, for a show of this complexity we got by with a 20-channel mixer. Years later, I'd get through twenty channels for the rhythm section alone. Once more, we were unable to group and the mix was final on quarter inch tape. No post production fiddling at that time (massive amount on that subject later!).

The band would take around twelve/thirteen channels. Two vocal microphones, two audience slung microphones and whatever was left over for the Max Jaffa strings, or extra audience microphones. The audience was just as important a facet as the show. So, that much hasn't changed over the years! You will see later (freelance section) that I would use eighteen audience microphones for Birds of a Feather at the Teddington Studios.

The sound crew for the Whitfield Show consisted of Jim Willis and myself. Jim was Head of Sound at that point. After the arduous rig, I would sit back and watch Jim mix the show. He was a cool guy, if Jim as much as shrugged it was a big gesture for him. He would never use two words when none sufficed.

Venue three was at Walthamstow Town Hall with a packed audience. During the break while the artistes were setting up for the second show, Jim beckoned to me to sit in the chair. *'This one is yours'* he said as he left the room. Wow!" Slung in at the deep end. This was my first location sound mix at Radio Luxembourg. I like to think it went well, anyway I didn't get the push!

Incidentally, Walthamstow Town Hall has remarkable acoustic qualities. Classical music makers were often recording choirs and big symphonic orchestras there. A couple more Town Hall auditoriums come to mind having good acoustical properties, certainly Watford Town and, if I remember correctly, Luton Town Hall, where I did the first in a series of Winifred Atwell Show. These building designs must have been flukes, I'm sure they weren't planned to be so in the thirties etc. Then again, perhaps many Town Halls throughout the land had always had good acoustical qualities. The Albert Hall was dreadful until the experts were called in.

THE DICKIE VALENTINE RADIO SHOW was the first programme that I recorded on our brand new, sleek Philips tape recording console. I insisted that Dickie with Geoff Love and his band come into the control room to inspect our pride and joy. They stood by dutifully while I explained the complexities of the machine. They feigned excited interest.

As the session drew to an end, the last song was halfway through when everything went silent. In the studio the band was playing, Geoff was conducting and Dickie was singing in his vocal booth. In sheer panic, I went to my new tape machine and inspected it closely. No input showed on the meters. About to stop the session, I suddenly heard a snigger – surely it came from the studio? Yes, it had. They had arranged to all stop playing and singing on a certain bar but to keep miming conning me into thinking my sleek new machine had malfunctioned.

They got me.

Several weeks later, I managed to get my own back on them during a late night session. After recording the final number well past ten at night, I told them I had a nasty tape jump owing to a bad edit and requested they go again. I told them I had to stand over the machine (out of their vision) and hold the tape against the head. I gave them the red light signal and while they were replaying the number (the original recorded version of which was perfectly okay) I quietly switched the equipment off then safely storing the recorded programme, I left a note asking them to turn the lights out and lock up. I then left via the front door. I think they took it well?

TOMMY TRINDER was very big even before the war. I can remember as a boy coming out of Mile End tube station and seeing him plastered all over billboards. His cheeky face and the slogan; 'Trinder's the name – YOU LUCKY PEOPLE'.

At Radio Luxembourg. We went on the road with *You Lucky People*. This was an audience show with the Norrie Paramour Band providing music between audience members coming on stage to win a token prize. Tommy never had a script and we never rehearsed.

One particular night at Poplar Town Hall in East London, because of fog, Tommy hadn't arrived from

Belgium where he had been watching his beloved Fulham football team (he was a director of the Club). Norrie entertained the waiting audience going through the band's repertoire. The audience was getting restless and producer Geoffrey Everett was about to cancel when Tommy, with suitcase, walked up the aisle from the front of the theatre. We rolled tape as he climbed onto the stage. Still carrying his suitcase he walked up to the microphone and said 'You Lucky People!' Norrie struck up with 'Hold That Tiger' (Tommy's signature tune) the show started and never stopped. Tommy was a very private person, we knew nothing of his home and personal life despite working with him for several months. I once heard him tell Geoffrey Everett that he had a fence put round his country house that cost two thousand pounds . . . in 1957!!

THE EDDIE CALVERT SHOW was another audience show recorded at different venues up and down the country for Radio Luxembourg. Eddie sometimes arrived late for a recording session. Undaunted, he would take his trumpet out of its case, give the band a one – two – three and without further ado go straight into his theme tune *'Cherry Pink & Apple Blossom White.* The trumpet 'slide' at the beginning was one of the most difficult things for a trumpeter to perform. Eddie was the consummate trumpet player. A very accomplished musician. Sam Cartmer mixed Eddie's shows and he always gave Sam five pounds after the event. Also a lot of dosh at that time. We shared it. For me a third of a weeks' pay.

Poplar Town Hall was used for recording the popular JOE LOSS Orchestra shows. These featured vocalists Ross McManus, Larry Gretton and Rose Brennan. Joe was a stickler for perfection until the clock started ticking too quickly and overtime loomed. He was a charming host to us all and when lunchtime neared he would send his manager to nearby Mile End to bring back forty salt beef sandwiches. Members of the saxophone section once confided to me that they dare not look at Joe's manic conducting whilst playing, as his shiny, black hair fell forward over his eyes. Joe was actually an astute business manager. There were not too many cruise ships plying the high seas at that time, but what few there were featured a 'Joe Loss Band'. Many cabaret stars also came from his agency.

MAX WALL was a Radio Luxembourg stalwart. We toured the country with his show *Laughter in Court* written by Tony Hawes. Max played a cod judge and members of the audience and cast were either in the witness box or the jury. Difficult to explain but it would have made a marvellous TV programme. Max had a fantastic sense of humour.

Tony Hawes (remember the *West End Tales* pub sequence?) later wrote stuff for the Bruce Forsyth Generation Game. He also did the voice over for the finale when contestants tried to remember the prizes rolling before them. Tony 'invented' the term . . . *'and a cuddly toy'* later in life, Tony took The Generation Game to South Africa, where he presented it himself.

On YouTube there is a super Des O'Connor rendering of a skit using a popular waltz where the names of just about every Hollywood film star, known and unknown is sung at breakneck speed;

'Hillary Brooke Elijah Cooke Sir C Aubrey Smith and Freddie Bartholomew' etc.

Try and check it out. This collage of words into song was collated by Tony Hawes.

In the afternoons before the evening performance of Laughter in Court, we would all gather in the hotel bar where Max Wall would relate a massive range of gags and stories, a different set for every hotel. Max was a superb raconteur. His career was sadly affected when he left his wife and umpteen kids to marry a Miss England (Violet Pretty, I think?). She used to sit in the front row during rehearsals, her eyes glued to Max, genuinely laughing at all his gags.

Max was very aware that all the guys' eyes were usually firmly fixed on his new bride. I doubt whether she even knew or cared.

***

15. More TV dramas . . .

NOT TO BE OUTDONE by the Light Entertainment output of Associated Television, the drama department could be relied upon to bring out their big guns. Laurence Olivier starred in both Long Day's Journey' and 'Uncle Vanya'. In this latter production I was a boom tracker and I well remember Mr. Olivier quietly prompting any of the cast who happened to either forget their lines or take too long delivering them. Being close to the action I could just hear his prompts. Presumably he did this on stage shows as well? His memory for dialogue must have been outstanding. The cast in 'Uncle Vanya' was awesome and often actors of the Michael Redgrave ilk took exception.

Often disdaining the waitress section, Sir Lawrence would queue for lunch along with everybody else holding animated conversations on any subject en route to the food counter. He had a cigarette brand named after him called *Olivier* (which I tried and quite liked) once he confided to me that if 'they' hadn't kept sending him 200 of the little ******** every week he would have given it up years ago. He wasn't frightened by a bit of ripe language.

H.M. Tennant Ltd. brought a drama into the studios weekly. These dramas brought the cream of British film and stage actors, not to mention the cream of television directors, capable of both directing artistes and having technical expertise in the control room. Quentin Lawrence, John Nelson Burton and a dozen others.

Some directors emanated from the theatre and were not so control room savvy – one such was Lionel Harris, a lovely man, idolised by the actors. In fact, an actor's director. After blocking the shots, he would sit back in the control room with his cat on his shoulder and watch as the vision mixer and the production assistant worked the show. It was as if he were seeing it for the first time.

I fondly remember the brilliant director, John Nelson Burton ripping the telephone off the wall when someone had the audacity to ring during dress rehearsal. John took over the directorial responsibility for a long running series set in the newspaper world called 'Deadline Midnight' – a Fleet Street drama series. It had gotten tired until John came in. He revitalised the cast, injecting masses of enthusiasm into the crew as if it were the pilot for a sensational new series.

The live transmission went extremely well, seemingly injected with a fireball. John came out of the control room on the gantry and addressed us all; *'Fantastic job everybody. I'm proud of you. Apart from a few cock-ups up here, bloody marvellous . . .'*

Getting a good performance from actors often required years of theatrical experience. Combining this to technical skills was rare. In the early days only John Nelson Burton, Dennis Vance, Quentin Lawrence and a couple others possessed this gift. The technical knowledge required to plot a shoot on a studio floor was daunting. With four cameras and three booms all connected by umbilical cords to wall points it was the director's task to organize their movements from set to set. A studio floor plan of the production had been provided by the designer and the director had to study this and work out how to get cameras and booms from one set to another without tangling cables. Often a daunting task which could take hours to work out. Very few directors had BOTH skills.

Anybody working for a period with John or the explosively, charming Dennis Vance has a tale to tell, for sure. Dennis had to 'stand in' for Blake Edwards for a Julie Andrews Special. Union rules dictated that Blake couldn't direct from the box. He passed his instructions to Dennis, who dutifully fulfilled the task until after once again being rebuffed with one of his own ideas, he hastily 'left' the control room, kicked a hole in a panel somewhere, letting off a few expletives before calmly returning to resume his task.

On retirement, Dennis, who had been a Fleet Air Arm pilot in the war, purchased a yacht (with his eighth wife) and did charters in the Med and Greek Islands. Anybody chartering his craft would have counted themselves most fortunate to be regaled from his massive store of anecdotes, especially after doses of vino mixed with midnight oil being burned. You may remember, Dennis did prison time for stabbing his PA. If there was ever a call for a biography, it would be Dennis Vance.

Three momentous episodes of NELSON starred Kenneth Colley. In episode three, the guns being fired on the mock gun deck in Studio C were not only heard in Studio D where I was Muppeting, but actually shook the floor and stopped production for a while. I believe this series was held up for transmission owing to the Falklands.

Sapphire & Steel starred David McCullum and Joanna Lumley and became cult viewing. *Goodnight & God Bless* was a six part series starring Donald Churchill. *Shine on Harvey Moon* starring Kenneth Cranham got us some exotic locations on the south coast of England.

Once, we had Kenneth Cranham rescuing his son from an incoming tide. Roger Wilkinson was working the pole up to his waist in water. After many takes the tide was coming in faster than anticipated. I knew Roger was not happy being immersed, he had to keep the pole aloft while the tide swirled around his chest. Suddenly he appeared to be in trouble - I yelled to him;

'For Pete's sake don't let the microphone get wet, Roger'

In the *Harvey Moon* studio, during a lunch break, a young Linda Robson used to sit in my sliding chair fiddling with my faders and using my talkback microphone proclaiming that this was a job she could do easily. I sound directed three series of Birds on a freelance basis (more about that later). Probably one of my happiest memories.

***

16. The Bing Crosby Christmas Specials.

THE CROSBY FAMILY had been making Christmas Specials in the United States for many years. However, in 1976, Bing came to ATV with his wife Kathryn, sons Gary and Nathaniel and daughter Mary, famed for her appearances in the hit soap Dallas.

Directed by Canadian Norman Campbell, the guest stars were a young and vibrant Bernadette Peters and a not so young and certainly not so vibrant Jackie Gleason. Bernadette sang a number unknown to us at that time, it was '*One (Singular Sensation)*' from the hit Broadway show *Chorus Line*. Her rendition was terrific.

Fake Christmas trees swamped the studio. Artificial snow was still being found weeks after the set was pulled down. An over-the-top Christmas tree-laden park area was designed for Bing and the entire family to wander around singing a cacophony of Christmas songs. It seemed apparent that none of the children had inherited Bing's vocal talents.

Gary played a nice guitar and in the obligatory Christmas medley none of the kids, or Kathy, disgraced themselves. Thankfully, because the medley was mimed, the listener avoided hearing whining snow machines swirling thousands of white chips of polystyrene around the studio.

Apparently, Bing wasn't the soul of generosity when it came to providing for his kids. Then again, perhaps he knew the pitfalls of giving Hollywood based children a free rein financially. Anyway, one morning Gary came up to the sound control room bursting with happiness. He had been given his 'fee' for the show and wanted to splash out on some hi-fi equipment. Where else to go but the sound guys? I passed him over to John Bain, my trusty number two. He enquired how much Gary had to splurge. Five hundred pounds said Gary excitedly. John explained that a good pair of speakers would make a big dent in that.

It was the middle of August and in the hottest year on record. The studio air conditioning could not be used during takes, so the dock doors were almost continually open to let some sort of fresh air in. 1976 was also the time when England played Australia in a series of gripping test matches. The vision department had rigged several floor monitors for the crew to follow the proceedings. The cast gathered round these monitors during breaks requesting explanations of the 'strange proceedings' taking place at Lords cricket ground. The scene boys were happy to oblige. Talks of 'leg before' and 'bowling a maiden over' caused sniggers from Mr. Gleason, who could well have been noting it all for future stag night speeches.

As Christmas shows go, our renowned Lord & Lady Grade's ATV kid's parties probably outshone most. This regular party was given to all the staff's kids. Lew wore a Father Christmas floppy hat and Lady Grade spent hours with the kids. Another ATV memory that will live in the minds of many.

The 1977 Bing Crosby *Merrie Olde Christmas* was a different kettle of fish. The Gary Smith/Dwight Hemion well-oiled production machine took over. Starring David Bowie, Stanley Baxter, Ron Moody, Twiggy, the Crosby Family and the Trinity Boys Choir.

The show opens with chauffer-uniformed Royce Mills delivering an invitation to Bing imploring him and the family to visit London to spend Christmas with his previously unknown British relative Sir Percy Crosby played in Bing Crosby style by Ron Moody.

The visit to Sir Percy's baronial mansion provided Messrs Baxter & Moody to adopt several parts Twiggy joined Ron Moody in a brilliant Christmas-past Dickensian sequence where they both also perform three different characters each. The *'Upstairs Downstairs'* scenario gave Stanley Baxter the opportunity to instruct Kathy Crosby in the downstairs culinary arts.

In another part of the show he did a Bob Hope impression that had Bing cracking up to such an extent he couldn't say his lines. Halfway through the show, David Bowie 'popped in' to sing *'Little Drummer Boy'* with Bing at the piano.

Several months later, a record company enquired whether the master sound tapes could be re-mixed to release a record in time for Christmas. I went to the sound store where the master tapes were kept to discover that the 16 track master sound tape had been erased. Head of Sound, Des Gray had authorised this because although not yet transmitted, the programme had been dubbed and was ready to air. I enquired why other programmes, some many years old, were still to be found in the store – no response.

As a result of this, the record company decided to use my on-line mix with Bing and David Bowie's voices picked up via the boom. The record had to be transcribed from a quarter inch tape recording that I had saved. They were able to use the video segment for television advertising, which boosted sales. It got to number one that Christmas, number two the following Christmas and still in the charts years later. It used to be customary to present the sound guy with a gold disc for a massive hit chart topper – I'm still around EMI?

Here's the clip that topped the charts for many years – only one take needed.

http://www.youtube.com/watch?v=gKTHvW2JcAA

The 45rpm sleeve – picture taken from the TV show.

The first day of sound recording for this show proved embarrassing for me. My number two, John Bain, had allowed young John Clark to do his job in the control room. Good experience for him, etc. After scanning the bandroom and checking mike placements while they were still rehearsing. Musical director, Ian Fraser then announced that they were ready to record the first song. This involved the whole Crosby family who were crowded into the vocal booth.

I rushed back upstairs, sat on my slider and started fading up the orchestra mike channels. Zilch! Nothing. Just *'shush'*. John Clark had inadvertently plugged up to studio D bandroom and not the main bandroom I quickly got John Bain up and we hastily re-plugged the jackfield. Meanwhile, Ian kept asking on talkback whether we were ready to go. He assumed we had heard the rehearsal and got our balance. After a several minutes, we finally got re-plugged but didn't dare ask for a run through.

Just my luck, they did the item in one take and in the confusion I never did get the percussion section. Something I had to 'fiddle with' in post-production. Microphones adjacent to the percussion area gave me some sort cover, but not too satisfactory.

Despite that one indiscretion, this was a happy shoot with Bing and the boys often disrupting a voice recording session because Nathaniel (a golfer heading for pro status) would come in to the vocal booth and say; *'Hey guys, it looks great out, let's go play golf'*.

The final song in the show was, of course, *'White Christmas'*. To our surprise, Bing wanted cue cards for the lyrics. Viewers will note he sings the first three lines live then, as the shot widens we go to the pre-recorded track.

Bing was a gentle, quiet man; patiently sitting with Kathryn in the beautiful lounge set designed by Henry Graveney, while Dwight gave instructions to the crew, or Johnny Rook fiddled with his lights. When I asked David Bowie whether I could put a tape echo in the *'Heroes'* song, he was hesitant until Bing assured him that it was safe in my hands. Although he sung live, the backing was his famous recorded track. The echo I added was on the backing only not his voice.

Buzz Kohan was the superb American writer whilst the Norman Maen dancers shone in the marvellous Dickens sequence on the back lot. This twenty minutes medley of Dickens characters brilliantly choreographed and performed, was the hi-light of the show. Settled snow, a gorgeously realistic set, horses and carts, a gaggle of geese all added to a showcase for the talents of Ron Moody and Twiggy.

Sadly, this was to be Bing's last ever show – he died on a golf course in Spain many weeks before Christmas. Kathryn Crosby prefaced the show on transmission to say that Bing had remarked that it was one of his happiest experiences and he was proud of the show.

For the aficionados;
Every television studio has several jack fields. Apart from access to dozens of microphone points and talkback distribution to the floor, the jackfield enables contact with other studios, band rooms, feeds to other control rooms and outside lines etc. A different jackfield will distribute talk back to the floor and elsewhere. Director's talkback will be separate from camera, sound and vision talkback systems. Programme sound and off-air sound will also be available to send to whoever requires it. For the uninitiated the jackfield can be a minefield. Hence John Clark's minor infraction.

***

17. Julie Andrews 'My Favourite Things'

FOR THIS PRODUCTION in 1975, Julie's husband, Blake Edwards, had got special permission to direct. The show started with a funny montage version of *"Favourite Things",* one of which was Julie eating a peanut butter sandwich whilst still singing. This she was unable to do and cracked up laughing. Blake kept this in the final cut.

With guest stars Peter Sellers and an early appearance of Jim Henson's Muppets, this was a very polished and entertaining programme (despite the bizarre occurrences after the initial shoot and subsequent additional shoot). Overall, it had a filmic look and this had to be due to Blake's interpretation. The 'special' guest star was The Pink Panther! Or, to be more precise, the four Pink Panthers performing a clever dance routine to the Pink Panther theme.

The show started with a tribute to Duke Ellington with Julie fronting the Jack Parnell Orchestra, then a clever dance sequence with the Jim Henson full-sized Muppets(rarely seen) involving vision control's expertise to 'blacken the set hiding the equally full-size Muppet operators. A musical item with Kermit was followed by a Peter Sellers comedy sketch.

Mr Sellers performed the sketch as a crazy German psychiatrist with a fixation on a Paddington Bear doll. Because of copyright problems, he was requested not to actually say the words Paddington Bear. This was a red rag to a bull!

The hilarious sketch, a third of which was ad libbed, resulted in Paddington Bear being heavily featured and mentioned. Weeks later, the entire sketch had to be re-shot in Hollywood, where the copyright problem did not exist. If you are a Peter Sellers fan, this is him at his zaniest. Blake wanted me to go to Los Angeles to oversee this sketch and the American post production. However, my head of department forbade it.

A highlight of FAVOURITE THINGS was the *'Flying down To Brighton'* sequence with some of the most ambitious choreography and set designs from Lewis Logan ever seen at the Elstree studios. The set piece was introduced by a comedic impression of 'Binkley Berkeley' (think Lew Grade) from Peter Sellers intimating that *'Anything Hollywood can do, we can do better'*. So *'Flying down To Rio'* is changed to *'Flying down To Brighton'*

It starts with Julie and the dancers on a mock up aeroplane wing before landing on Brighton Beach. The whole sequence culminates with Julie dressed in a terrific all-white naval outfit dancing a nautical compilation on board a battleship with Paddy Stone's twenty four dancers. (At artiste's world rates, this was an extravagance). The multi-dancing precision is something not seen too often these days, especially when shot in a filmic fashion, something Blake could do in his sleep.

This is a Julie Andrews classic. Dressed in an all-white nautical outfit, I doubt Julie has ever looked more lovely. The show ends (rather tamely) with Julie singing 'Melancholy baby' to camera in close-up. A wrap was announced and the studio was cleared. But Blake was not happy.
Apparently, some days before, he and Julie had gone out to the wilds of Essex to view the fabulous stone artistry of Sir Henry Moore. They were very taken with the gigantic

statues to be found in the capacious grounds of the museum-like home of Henry Moore.

Now, sitting in the control room as the studio was clearing, Blake suggested that he wanted to take the crew out to Sir Henry Moore's residence and shoot a number with Julie. Production Manager, Billy Glaze told Blake that was simply not a runner. The show was over, finished, kaput. Knowing Billy, a few expletives were inserted here and there. The decision was passed to studio chief, Dennis Bassinger was more polite but the same answer. The show was completed, and on time, and further work could not be countenanced.

Blake, unperturbed at this rebuttal, picked up a telephone and rang Sir Lew Grade. At that time negotiations were going on for another Pink Panther movie for Lew. He gave Blake permission to do practically anything he wanted and the necessary arrangements were put in place.

Musical director, Ian Fraser, hastily got together a trio to accompany his piano and within the hour Julie was laying down a guide track to 'Out Of This World' The contention being that she would wander around the modernistic statues intimating that they were literally out of this world.

Next morning, a Saturday, the crew (on short notice overtime) started to arrive at 0630. A huge filmic camera crane had already been delivered and eventually Bill Brown, the senior cameraman, sat atop this giant with Blake Edwards alongside. They were looking for shots.

We played bits of the track on loudspeakers involving massive cable runs while Julie traversed the huge statues singing first one line, then stop, then move the camera and equipment to another location, another statue, then another line of song, then stop again while another shot was searched for. The haste with which the shoot had been put together had not allowed for a cohesive camera plan. This went on until well after lunchtime.

Apart from the usual bacon sandwich breakfast, a catering truck had prepared lunch for something like sixty people. At half past three in the afternoon, Julie was looking fragile. After trekking yet another two hundred yards to a possible site, then that site being rejected, she turned to Blake and said;

'Blake, I'm bushed'.

Blake turned to floor manager Richard Holloway and said;

'Call a wrap, Richard'.

We wrapped with half the sequence unfinished. The catering truck does a roaring trade! Arrangements were made to have a couple of the statues low-loaded to Elstree the following Monday where it was discovered the studio floor was unable to take the weight. The statues were placed on the lawn outside the office block, and that afternoon Julie finished the sequence.

All this gave the impression that the Blake Edwards art of 'filming a sequence' is not as cost effective as 'videoing a sequence'. We all looked forward to seeing the edited version when we prepared for the post production sound dub. Bizarrely, the item was never used. 'Melancholy Baby' was restored as the finale. Blake had dumped it on the 'cutting room floor'. Why? I never got to know. Had I gone to the States for the post I would have found out. Then again, Blake, being a filmic person with years of experience, was quite used to shooting lots of stuff then choosing later on the edit to discard footage irrespective of how much it cost to shoot in the first place. The term 'cutting room floor' started and largely remained in the film industry. Any ATV director going down that road would soon find themselves in hot water. The imposing (and often frightening) figure of Bill Ward would come down on them like a ton of bricks.

None the less, Julie Andrews MY FAVOURITE THINGS was probably one of the best light entertainment shows to emit from the Elstree Studios in the nineteen seventies.

There are clips of this super show on YouTube. I have an old beaten up version taken from the original videotape then copied a few times and a few times more. Now, I can see most of my stuff on YouTube in much better quality.

***

18. The Muppet Years.

LORD LEW GRADE, that entrepreneur extraordinaire, had the brilliant idea to bring Jim Henson's Muppet characters to Elstree for a series after the American networks had rejected the idea. Jim had previously brought his Muppet team to Elstree for inserts into other American aimed productions, of which *Julie on Sesame Street* was by far the best.

Many top writers were employed for the first series of *The Muppet Show* produced by Smith and Hemion and overseen by the American comedian/producer stalwart Jack Burns. The directors for the series were Peter Harris (ATV staff) and Phillip Casson (freelance). Writer Jack Burns sat alongside the director for the entire first series and attended all dubbing sessions.

Jack was a brilliant personage. On show one, when Gonzo announced he was going to eat the entire car on set, even the tyres . . . Jack stopped the recording and got Gonzo to add the words (after a pause) . . . *'white walls'.* As if that was the ultimate task. However, Jack was a volatile person. On one dub he insisted on a big laugh after Fozzie Bear while ordering a meal added; *'Hold the mayo'*. I queried this with Jack asking if it were funny. He exploded, left the dubbing suite and didn't come back for two hours. An example of the differences between American and British humour.

Once, in a phone call a secretary innocently gave Jack's ex-wife his forwarding address – this compelled Jack to leave the country. His whereabouts unknown, he resurfaced a couple of weeks later having moved hotels.

After the first series, Jim Henson decided to do without Jack's assistance (and Gary & Dwight's) for the rest of the memorable five years of Muppetry. However, Jack Burns came back a year later to produce (and star in) a terrific crazy series called BONKERS but more of that later.

Sound-wise, I did the first two Muppet pilot shows after which Roger Knight and I alternated for most of the remainder of the five year run. Each show took around five days to shoot and we had a weekly turn round.

On week one – Monday; the music was recorded in the band room with the guest star. After lunch, Muppet voices would then be added to the musical items with the regular Muppet operators. This usually took until 8 pm. Laughter emanated from the vocal booth on many occasions. One item was totally sung in bubbles and gargles (*'Gargling Gershwin'*). The operators would drink a glass of water and gargle along with the track. Some of these sessions would have provided a show on their own.

On the *Muppet Show* No artiste was permitted to bring their own musicians. You used the Muppet band and staff arrangers or didn't do the show. Some artistes failed this condition, I think Barbara Streisand certainly qualified for that – but then Babs would have wanted to direct it as well not to mention operating Kermit at the same time.

The Muppet band, under the direction of Jack Parnell, was a nine piece comprised of the best session musicians of the day. The LP of the show came from stuff that Roger

Knight and I had recorded at the studios over the first year, or so. We were both presented with a gold disc by Jim. One number *Halfway up the Stairs* sung by Jerry Nelson playing Kermit's little brother actually topped the charts as a single.

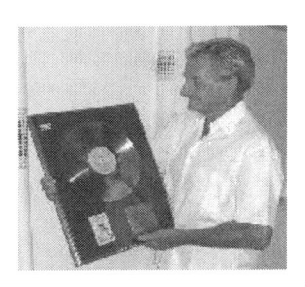

Both Roger Knight and I were presented with a gold disc of the musical items from the show. Chosen from well over five hundred songs.

The Muppet Show guest stars were met at the airport, limo'd to the studio and given the TOP STAR treatment by the Henson Organization's own production star, David Lazer, who could, and did, charm the wings off a bird without batting an eyelid. A Royal welcome with a constant smile was David's trademark.

Shooting-wise, Tuesday was 'Guest Star' day. The artiste would do a sketch, or two, sing a song or two and say the farewell speech in front of the tabs. Live voice was picked up from the artiste via a boom whilst the Muppet Operators (out of vision) had head-sets and microphones for dialogue.

On camera, the artiste usually stood on a raised platform with the operators beneath them working their dolls whilst following the action on a small TV sets scattered around the floor. The Muppet set-up was such that the camera team used two Mole cranes. A basic camera dolly could handle heights of six feet but the Muppet characters were always several feet higher.

Whilst Roger Moore was charming the pants off Miss Piggy on a sumptuous sofa, Frank Oz would be squeezed in under that sofa while watching the picture output on a monitor, manipulating Miss Piggy while following a script. I can think of no better way to describe the talents of Frank Oz than to offer this clip. Later in the clip is the entire Roger Moore, Miss Piggy epic. Roger interacted with the Muppets to perfection. This is among my favourite Muppet Shows.

Other situations involved multi muppets. A good example comes to mind with the PAUL SIMON Muppet Show. He performed *'Strawberry Fair'* walking and singing live among rows of stalls with Muppet characters selling all types of market produce. The stalls would be at camera level while Paul walked a narrow plank between them. Six feet beneath the plank would be a cacophony of power and talkback cables feeding the monitors and operators.
Interestingly, after a playback of the Paul Simon Muppet Show, Richard Hunt (Scooter) was overheard saying to Jerry Nelson (Dr Strangepork and Crazy Harry), *'He should have brought Art'*. Operators like Richard Hunt and Gerry Nelson were multi-talented because apart from being top puppet manipulators they also gave each of their characters a memorable voice and KEPT to it for the entire series. Louise Gold was the British puppeteer alongside Jim Henson, Frank Oz, Dave Goeltz and Steve Whitmire, who later was to become the new Kermit the frog. Only to lose that distinction in 2018 when the Henson Organization decided a new Kermit voice was required.

Louise Gold operated a smaller (and younger) pig than Miss Piggy causing much humorous, well written friction. The lovely Louise could easily have been a big star in the musical world. Recently, she was a lead in MAMA MIA. A recent meeting (2018) revealed that Louise is starring in a massive NETFLIX re-make of *Dark Crystal* the Jim Henson classic. Can't wait to see that. Frank Oz, of course, later became a famous movie director after Jim tragically died.

Director Peter Harris was a great influence on the shows. His liaison with Jim was exceptional. Jim wasn't the type to accept too much 'advice' (far from it). It was his show, his concept (and his life) at all times, but he did listen to Peter constantly. Peter continued in the puppet director frame for many years from Spitting Image to all sorts of other Henson inspired productions. In five years of the Muppet Show, Bonkers and a few Specials, what with re-takes and rehearsals, I estimate that Peter Harris turned to me from the gallery over five thousand times and said; . . . *'Cue the tape please, Ted'.* This is another clip showing the writers (over lunch) with Jim narrating and Frank Oz joining in. Later some classic Muppet moments.

http://www.youtube.com/watch?v=H0v2D46qaRA

Roger Knight, with crew 1 did all of his Muppet Shows with director Phillip Casson while I usually worked with Peter Harris. Phil continued his career as a jobbing director, music, drama, you name it – he could put his hand to anything, even having a beautiful boat built in Taiwan and driving it home with wife and children. Where are you now Phil?

Because the UK had less commercial breaks than other countries, every UK Muppet Show had a 'two minute spot' – the space had to be filled with a song, usually a UK based item (*Any old iron etc*). Incidentally, the two minutes had to be frame accurate EXACTLY. This always involved tricky work by ace VTR editor, John Hawkins. The sound dub was an important factor. Sometimes a show would require a hundred, or so sound effects to be laid onto the track in synch. Because Roger and I often worked on small segments of The Muppet Show that would be banked and appear in a later show, kit was imperative e that we use the same tracking for storage of music and dubbing tactics.

The eight track dubbing recorder was configured as follows;

Track 1. Main edited program sound.

2-3-4 Music & dialogue laid back from sound studio master recorders.

5-6 laughter and applause tracks

7-8 Final mix (ready for layback to VTR and buzz track to enable perfect synchronization.

Sixteen track recorders were later used improving the storage problems.

As in all ATV shows at that time, it was imperative that all post production sound was laid back to the video tape. Without that facility, sound could be fifth, or even sixth generation. (See BOB HOPE GALA NIGHT later).

The laughter dub was time consuming. Every added laugh (and they were ALL added) involved a debate. Jim and Frank attended all dubs and ensured that the laughter chosen for any gag was correct. My job was to mix the whole thing together for a finished show ensuring (at all times) that no dialogue was drowned by laughter or added effects. Today (as I may have touched upon before!) I often sit dejected in front of my telly deploring the lack of finesse in voice to music mixing.

Re-takes during the dub were multiple. Sometimes an added laugh was too short, too long, too raucous, not raucous enough etc - we would wind back time and time again, drop into record and try it once more. This always occurred after a long track laying day when Jim and Frank would appear and the final dub mix would commence. An easy show would be finished by ten thirty. A difficult show could go well into the early hours.

The remainder of the dub week would involve producing the various other versions for world consumption. Muppet Show recording week was a five day affair. The second week for dubbing and world versions would be three and a half days. This careful (and miserly) scheduling would involve no overtime payments for the Muppet sound crews but we were proud to be an important part of a production that would be seen in a hundred countries around the world.

A word about the laughter machine is relevant. This machine was devised by ATV's Design & Maintenance department (our Mission Control) after consultations with the sound department chiefs and Indians. It had sixteen faders all loaded with a different function. Two faders held coughs. The others had laughs of varying degrees from chuckles to bigger chuckles to even bigger chuckles to small laughs to slightly bigger laughs to much bigger laughs. Applause could be started on one fader, continuous on another and ended on another. Other bands of applause of set lengths were also loaded.

All fingers on both hands could be doing different things with this machine and, on the whole, it worked well. Jim often said he would prefer to have done the show without a laugh dub but the Networks in the USA could not countenance that scenario. One Muppet Show had the guest star (Steve Martin) arriving as the theatre was supposedly being redecorated. Without the Muppet audience, Jim foresaw this as a 'no laugh track' production. But it was not be to be, the Network big wigs clamped down.

To operate this 'laughter-machine monster', no amount of schooling could be provided. You may have ten 'A' levels and be useless. We had our sound technician, Roger Banks (remember Stringbean from the Peter Pan segment?) For some obscure reason Roger had the knack. You had to be pretty odd to work this machine successfully and Roger filled that position with consummate ease.

He had a good (but often strange) sense of humour and he made the machine laugh along with himself. If Roger considered something not funny, the machine wouldn't laugh and he had to be convinced it WAS funny. If he went off track, he would willingly go again, and again. He never lost his cool, never (ever) argued with Jim or

Frank or me but managed to do things with that machine that few others got close to.

There were over a hundred and thirty Muppet Shows, of which I was sound director on almost a half. Roger Knight, the other sound director, probably has his top ten favourites but mine were roughly as follows;
    Elton John;
    Buddy Rich;
    Star Wars;
    Ethel Merman;
    Liza Minelli;
    Roger Moore;
    Johnny Cash;
    Debbie Harry;
    Juliet Prowse and Rita Moreno.

The Rita Moreno Muppet Show featured her singing *Fever* (the Peggy Lee classic). The backing Muppet band had Animal behind his drum kit in shot. In every pause Animal broke into a drum lick annoying Miss Moreno intensely. Eventually she stops singing walks to the drum kit, produces two huge cymbals and crashes them into Animal's head. He responds; *'That's my kinda woman'.*

I am always amazed at the number of people in America who thought the Muppet Show was made in their country. It was, of course, made in Elstree. The adjacent studio C band room was converted to the Muppet workshop. Here dozens of Muppets were constantly being made, cleaned, restored and duplicated. There were several Kermits, Miss Piggys' and Fozzie Bears. The shoot went from 0930 to 2000. Not a second past that time was permitted by stringent union rules. Thus, the red lights were on all day and usually ignored. To burst in when something was actually being recorded would be a rare event, but invoked a lot of bad studio discipline.

When Buddy Rich arrived, they had the idea to have the electricity in the Muppet Theatre to be on the blink. When Buddy was challenged to a drum duel by Animal, the little monster in desperation at being outdone by Buddy chucks a drum over his head, hence the reason for Buddy to say;

'There go those lights again'.

There is a YouTube clip highlighting the extraordinary talent of Frank Oz doing Animal's drum battle, miming meticulously to Ronnie Verrell's live off-stage drumming.

I think the most boring day I recollect on any Muppet Show was on the Leo Sayer show. The entire studio floor was covered with grass, trees, bushes and shrubs. All built several feet higher so that muppet operators could work beneath the surface, where a multitude of monitors and cables were to be found. Leo was to be discovered up a tree singing *'When I need love'* as a bear was trying to climb that tree. All around, muppet animals were poking their heads out of rabbit holes etc. These apertures took many hours to devise, but Jim often wanting the hole in the grass to be somewhere else. Or, the holes had to be enlarged (or shrunken) to accommodate a different Muppet.

That day I think we only shot 38 seconds! It was a memorable number, one of my favourites, but with that shooting ratio, they'd still be doing *'War and Peace'* to this day! Since those halcyon Muppet Years at Elstree the Henson Organisation have made feature films and even regurgitated new versions of the show itself, but I think somehow . . . . The original wins!

I had the good fortune, when in Los Angeles to meet Henry Winkler and he expressed a great desire to do a Muppet Show. I envisaged the muppets walking around combing their hair etc, as Henry was known to do in his popular TV show *Happy Days*. On returning to Elstree, I mentioned this to Jim, convinced he would be keen to get him. But Jim just gazed in to the distance and said; '*Oh really?*' - Nothing came of it.

In the present day world of puppetry, rarely does the puppet operator do the voice, i.e. *Spitting Image* – where the voice is provided by an impersonator which the puppet operator had to learn and synchronize to.

ATV already had a massively successful and long running show called INIGO PIPKINS, which called for the operators to not only manipulate the puppet but to use their own voices thereby giving the puppet a trademark sound.
BIRMINGHAM PIG and HARTLEY HARE spring to mind. The show starred George Woodbridge as the human being link person. The show transformed to PIPKINS after George died. Most of the shows were directed by Michael Jeans and the main puppet operator (and voice) was Nigel Plaskitt (and voice) these days a renowned puppet wrangler.

***

19. More ATV memories.

THE SURE FIRE WINNER of an award would surely be the late 1970's productions *Julie on Sesame Street*. Smith and Hemion had just finished shooting *Barbra Streisand and Other Musical Instruments* in Studio C before immediately moving into studio D for Julie's Sesame Street Special. The Streisand team were equally sure they were bound to win.

The Streisand show was probably the finest production to ever come out of Elstree. This kaleidoscope of music and musicians from all around the world was brilliantly woven together to highlight Ms Streisand's talents. My friend, the late Bill Nuttall, sound directed the show and, apart from his superb musical mixing, his computer sound item before the days of digital computerization is still astounding.

    Next door in D, we were preparing for Julie and her guest star Perry Como visiting the famous Sesame Street set. Their twenty minute duet (The Sing Medley) took a day to record. Dwight Hemion edited the medley by cutting ten frames here, twenty frames there – all in all about sixty edits. To relay the audio in perfect synch, tape operator Dave Pull had to make the same edits on quarter inch which would then be used to relay the sound onto the final VTR master. This was a momentous task. However, Dave knew the medley quite well as he had previously boom operated the sequence. Dave epitomised the strange qualities that television brought out in people in those earlier days. Guys like him adapted to a job that provided no training. Dave Pull epitomised the perfect talented sound guy. Another example of you've either got it or you haven't.

Another great boom op was Roy Nilsen, who was previously a merchant seaman. Roy would zoom in for a close-up then whip out sharply for the wide shot, often frightening the life out of the artiste (and probably the vision mixer too?). The skilled boom operator is in decline owing to the advent of hidden radio mics and the recording of sequences in small chunks.

Like dozens of others, *Emergency Ward Ten* was a live half hour soap that relied upon boom operators keeping out of shot and avoiding boom shadows while keeping the artiste on mic. Often you were tracked from scene to scene with seconds to spare before racking out.

I well remember operating a boom on Roy Orbison, who had a notoriously 'small' voice. I was partially in shot most of the time on the bumpy track as Mr. Orbison walked from one end of studio C to the other. Director Albert Locke kept shouting *'boom in'* as sound director Bill Nuttall kept retorting *'keep it there'* – you don't make many friends among the camera department with that sort of scenario.

I had a similar situation with a Lonnie Donnegan show where it was ordained a boom should be used where a stand mike would have been better. In the long shot I was constantly in a cameraman's shot. Being told by my sound director to 'keep it there' I stayed in shot for the entire item. Not madly in shot but bending the top five lines. The cameraman, who lived quite close to me, didn't speak to me for nearly a year.

Perry Como knew the pitfalls of boom operating from his hit series in the States. He often waited (without letting on) to deliver a line while the boom 'got there'.

During the Sesame Street shoot, Perry brought his grandchildren up to the control rooms, and his cool easy going manner disguised the fact that he also knew control rooms backwards.

The Sesame Street Show was entered it for the American TV Awards that year. Barbra Streisand's Special was also entered, secretly I thought it would beat us. Neither got to the finishing post, it was won by a cool, easy going singer who hosted *the Perry Como Show.*

In the following clip, from *Julie on Sesame Street* the mammoth medley was shot in two takes. Halfway through, Julie's voice was louder than Perry's, despite Dave Pull star boom operator favouring Perry. A radio mic was fitted, but even then Julie's voice was often louder than Perry's through his added microphone. A tricky post mix.

STEVE LAWRENCE & EYDIE GORME did two Specials highlighting the music of George Gershwin and Cole Porter. The Gershwin show starred GENE KELLY. One segment was shot in Paris and the concert spot featured a sixty piece orchestra playing live to accompany Steve & Eydie.

Their terrific Gershwin medley which, I gather, was the mainstay of their Vegas act. I have this show on VHS, one of my musical favourites. The Concert Spot was the first thing we shot for the programme. We rigged the set for the sixty piece orchestra using something like forty microphones. The set was a mock-up of the Eiffel Tower (Paris – Gershwin being the theme of the show).

Ten minutes before lunch, Nick Perito, the musical director having just flown in from the States that morning, popped in and was horrified to see we had put the string section on the left of the set. He explained that he played piano and conducted during the spot and would have preferred them on the right, facing him. We switched the strings around with the saxophones and brass, nearly an hour's work and he was quite chuffed.

When he returned to the States, he rang me to request a quarter inch copy of the Concert Spot. This was done. A couple of weeks later he rang again to say the tape I had sent him contained forty minutes of bird and parrot effects. Whoops! A switch of cassettes from the sound effects library was responsible.

Steve & Eydie were a dream team. So professional, Eydie had perfect pitch and I put Steve Lawrence in the Frank Sinatra top-of-the-tree range. Their microphone technique was first class. I gave them Sennheiser C41 hand microphones with in-built windshields. I DETEST big, black windshields that are so often used.

The Concert Spot was the entire middle third of the show. We did it in two takes. From my point of view the first take was the best. But Dwight Hemion used bits from each in the final cut. After recording the first take, the orchestra were given a tea a break while Steve and Eydie went up to the gallery to watch a playback. We retired to the canteen for our usual tea and buns. After ten minutes Eydie Gorme came into the canteen and asked someone which was the sound table. She came over to us and said;

'Just wanna say to you guys, that's the best Goddam live orchestra sound ever . . .' with that she turned and left.

One of the sound guys remarked; *'You'd have thought she would have stood us a tray of teas?'*

The medley with Gene Kelly was mostly live vocal; foot-taps were picked up by a roving floor Sennheiser. This show was nominated for something-or-the-other but I don't think it scored?

The Cole Porter follow-up starred ETHEL MERMAN and BOB HOPE. The concert spot was similar to the Gershwin but the music was pre-recorded and although Steve & Eydie still sung live, it lacked 'buzz'.

Eydie mysteriously lost her voice just before the Cole Porter medley to be performed with Ethel Merman in a clever mock-up of the *'Dale Carnegie library'* set thanks to Designer Brian Holgate. Eydie was reluctant to perform but to avoid shoot time loss; she was persuaded to mime her portion of the medley (some eighteen minutes long) because Ethel was due to fly out. She sang her parts at normal level as if it was what she normally did, while Eydie mimed hers.

Later that week, Eydie (now just as mysteriously recovered) came into the dubbing suite where we had a television monitor for her to watch the medley while she actually sang the mimed parts. To our astonishment, she did the entire medley in one take. Eydie Gorme, one of the finest singers to come out of the United States.

The Muppet season took long summer breaks when all the operators went home to their California pads. Enter the Summer Replacement Show. The American networks had holes to fill and wanted them filled cheaply. No big names, no big writers, just footage. *Bonkers* was one of the shows that filled this slot and it looked like being a turkey long before Christmas came around.

Our odd-ball friend JACK BURNS played the part of the producer of the show. He didn't have a UK Equity ticket so he decided to wear a 'Lone Ranger' type face mask to avoid recognition! The whole show was crazy. At one point, a mock volcano used as a backdrop to a production number caught fire. Security rushed on to quell the small blaze while Jack pushed them off, saying *'don't worry guys, we're heavily insured'* this was all ad lib and kept in the show.

Muppet director Peter Harris kept Jack on a tight rein. American producer Tom Battista devised a series of sketches for the Hudson Brothers to re-enact the Ritz Brother routines. These very clever sketches were heavily laden with sound effects and Tom showed us he knew his onions in that field.

Apart from being professional comedians, the Hudson Brothers were also a rock group and they did a series of Concert Spots with an audience. Having brought their backing band over from the US (Tom arranged cheap fares) we had a ball recording the Hudson's with their band. After we wrapped, I buzzed off home while my Aussie number two, Dave McNally did multi-track playbacks for the group in sound control. I understand, they went on until the early hours or until the beer ran out.

I was glad that Dave played host to the Hudson's in the control room playbacks. I had previously had a slight altercation with Bill Hudson when they first arrived in the studio. He wanted a certain type of microphone for all their musical items whilst I was proud to offer him a new design that was smaller and better quality. Also, my choice would be without ugly black windshields a sore point with me. Not only that, we didn't possess the microphone he preferred. They had gone to be laid to rest at ATV Birmingham.

No, Bill was adamant, he wanted his choice. We 'discussed' back and forth until Tom Battista intervened. I got my way but not before asking them when they were going to have a similar discussion with the camera department regarding lens usage and the vision department as well for the choice of cameras? I made my point.

One lunch break, in the queue, I had the pleasure of tickling the cheek of the new-born baby belonging to Bill Hudson and Goldie Hawn. Wonder if Kate Hudson remembers that?

BOB MONKHOUSE was the British component of *Bonkers*. The Hudson's kept calling him 'monkey'. Bob would scream don't call me monkey, which became something of a catch-phrase. One regular spot had Bob doing a lengthy monologue during which he would inevitably say the words 'ball'. At this point a wrecking ball swung in and knocked him flying. This was a running gag.

On a dress rehearsal of the last show, Bob ad-libbed a very lengthy, quick-fire routine discussing house demolishing and the machinery required to achieve this without once mentioning wreck or ball. The Hudson's loved it, and him. Bob told me he enjoyed this series more than any game show he hosted. Our 'turkey' was turning into a gourmet meal.

Mark Hudson fell for one of the dancers (Wendy) and they got married back in Hollywood. The very handsome Brett Hudson largely kept himself to himself concentrating on his guitar (that's his story and he's sticking to it!). Bill Hudson (now divorced from Goldie) turned out years later, virtually unrecognizable, to be something of a weirdo, wearing strange outfits and appearing on various chat shows.

Early in the ten part series, Jack Burns went to see *Evita* in London and took a liking to Elaine Paige (to put it mildly!). Apparently, he saw the show a dozen times paying an arm and a leg to ticket touts. Desperately, he tried to get Elaine into Bonkers but the American sponsors wanted names and Elaine, at that time, didn't fit that bracket.

He did finally manage it and Elaine had a big production number that Jack thought might be funny if a dozen doves flew in at the end. Fly in they did and tried to settle on Elaine's hair.

She was not best pleased and hastily returned to the serenity of *Evita*. A terrific fun show for the crews, Bonkers did go out in the UK, whether it ran the full series, I know not. Being non-Equity, the appearance of Jack Burns would have caused a problem.

The heyday of ATV's musical specials were never entirely devoted to the US market. *HMS Pinafore* was a particular highlight. With a fifty piece orchestra the entire Doyle Carte Company pre-recorded the musical items in Studio C. Later that week, the set was constructed and the artistes performed the perennial favourite miming the tracks and performing the dialogue live with impeccable perfection.

From a sound perspective, the transition from mimed song to spoken dialogue was perfect. An audience of staunch Gilbert & Sullivan devotees ensured a happy production. On *the* music record session, a new recruit joined the crew, one Roger Banks (Yes, *Stringbean* again!). Roger watched the recording through the sound control window, conducting and singing along with the lyrics. Hello, hello, I thought, we've got an odd one here. I wasn't wrong. The ATV version of Doyle Carte's *HMS Pinafore* is available commercially on VHS and DVD. Try and spot which is mimed/live!

ANN-MARGRET recorded two Specials, *Ann-Margret Olson* and (when she married) *Ann-Margret Smith*. This highlighted the art works of Andy Warhol. One sketch featured the hilarious SID CAESER taking the part of Toulouse le Trec (on his knees). He asked Ann in heavy French accent for a loan saying; *'I'm a little short today'.* She replied in even heavier cod French; *'Huh! You are a little short **every** day'.*

Why is it that remains with me more than forty years later? There's a terrific video clip of Ann-Margret singing and dancing *'That's when the music takes me'* She roars into the studio on a Harley Davidson – wouldn't be allowed today under 'health & safety' – it would be pushed in having had its petrol tank emptied, rather spoiling the choreography.

Ann-Margret was as lovely as she looks. At the wrap she handed out magnums of champagne. We still have the bottle (regretfully, empty!)

DUSTY SPRINGFIELD came to ATV at the height of her fame. Her avid interest in the audio aspect of the show was evident from the number of hand written notes that she used to send imploring me to dip the strings at bar 12, enhance the choir over her voice level during the coda and other musical instructions.

Called to her dressing room once, while being made-up, and with eyes closed, she went through the entire show virtually sound mixing it herself. On the rare occasion when she mimed a track and had a tricky pick-up, her out-stretched hand would momentarily come between her mouth and the camera lens, covering any discrepancy. Clever girl was Dusty and a great performer. She was very aware of the importance of a television appearance. She told me of the importance of allowing an orchestral piece to occasionally exceed the level of the singer, how burying the singer in with the choir could be more effective. Once, over-hearing Lulu tell a fellow performer not to worry about the sound, as it was 'only' television, I felt obligated to pop down on the floor and influence that opinion more in my favour. Lulu was very gracious considering my eavesdropping cheek.

CHARLIE DRAKE came to ATV from the BBC in a series called *'Who Is Sylvia'* directed by Shaun O'Riordan. This was shortly after Charlie had been injured in a sketch being thrown through a bookcase and left unconscious. Rumour had it that the floor guys at the beeb had just about had enough! Whether that's true I don't know. Also rumoured was that they nick-named him 'the orange dwarf'.

Charlie was okay with us. During camera rehearsal he sat in a director's chair with a telephone to both Shaun in the gallery and to me in sound control. As the show was being rehearsed (with a Charlie Drake stand-in) he would give directorial tips to Shaun and often telephoned me requesting a sound effect, or similar. *'I think a clap of thunder would be appropriate here Edward?'* (Often he would say *'ere Hedward'* whether in jest, or not, I never figured out). Charlie always called me Edward, and everybody always called him Charles.

The floor manager was Paul Knight who later became executive producer of the successful film series *Black Beauty.* Young Paul was well over six feet tall and Charlie probably felt intimidated. Paul was replaced by Pat Richards (well under six feet). Poor old Shaun O'Riordan, the director had to give in to many of Charlie's whims.

Many years later, totally out of the blue, Charlie crept into sound control while we were doing a Muppet Show. Not seen on telly for years he had found his way to sound control with a mission. Apparently his budgerigar had stopped talking to him. Charlie's re-telling gave the impression that this was nothing short of a calamity. Thus, Charlie wanted a budgie talking from our sound effects library to try and 'gee' his little birdie up. He described his budgie with lots of (silent) mimicking and hand gestures, we wondered if he was being serious, or is he just having us on? Still keeping the talent happy we naturally obliged. While waiting for his tape from sound effects, Charlie watched a scene being rehearsed of the Muppets without giving any indication. He appeared in a different world.

The Reg Varney series was directed and produced by William G. Stewart. His proud boast was that despite starting from the lowly ranks of a scene shifter he would hitch himself to star to become famous himself. Well, he certainly did that by becoming a star in *'Fifteen to One'* which he devised, and produced. Not to mention earlier producing the massive hit series *The Price Is Right* with Leslie Crowther.

Reg Varney played a mean piano and that facet of his talent was, to him, more important than the comedic angle. After the outside rehearsal, which all the crew heads attended, Reg would corner me and play his two musical items on the old rehearsal room piano, often hitting the wooden bit at the end of the high notes in his enthusiasm. Reg had a perennial smile and a charming manner. Apparently, he was also a very fine artist, oils and water colour.

Another keen pianist, also more concerned with his musical performance was Dudley Moore. During the ATV Pete n'Dud series his concern over the mixing of his group was paramount. Dudley was a very fine musician and had not a Hollywood career beckoned, his musical talent could easily have propelled him into the book of jazz greats, if not already there.

Recording a piano sounds simple? Just bung a microphone into the well, right? Well, a lot depends on the piano and many other factors. There must be hundreds of beautifully recorded piano pieces available for the aficionado, for sheer quality recorded perfection I love Vladimir Ashkenazi playing Rachmaninov's second piano concerto with the Concertgebouw conducted by Bernard Haitink, the reproduction of the bass end of the piano is quite extraordinary. Out of many dozens of contenders, my second choice of piano perfection is Dudley Moore's haunting album '*A Genuine Dud*' (great title). The double bass and drum sounds are superb.

Pianist RUSS CONWAY appeared on many ATV shows at Wood Green Empire and Elstree studios. His repertoire appeared to consist of half dozen items usually of ragtime nature. He was extremely popular with the audience. I recollect Russ being very nervous, literally shaking in the wings before emerging on stage to give a flawless performance. Russ was another performer with a winning smile. Obviously Liberace had quite an influence on pianists. Although on reflection, I don't remember Dave Brubeck smiling too much on his Sunday Night at the London Palladium appearance. I wonder what all the above would have made of Lang Lang? Lots of Liberace there with bucket loads of added talent. How do these people memorise all the masterpieces they play with such consummate ease? I often can't remember where I was last week.

PETULA CLARK starred in a marvellous drama/music Special called *Traces of Love* with Paul Jones, David Kernan and the Norman Maen Dancers. Directed by Jon Scoffield, Traces was shot in several very long sequences almost always in one take. This was a strain for the crew, get it right first time or Jon would exude wrath usually via a withering look or devastating sarcasm. I never had a cross word with Jon and he always allowed me massive latitude in the dubbing suite where I always tried to add a spot of signature tape echo or something 'unusual'.

Roy Simper's camera crew were, as always, impeccable. Make-up-wise, I don't think Petula has ever looked better thanks to Mary Southgate. Pet's musical director Kenny Clayton, arranged all the music and conducted the Jack Parnell Orchestra for the recording session before jetting off to south America where he would set up Pet's forthcoming concert. Richard Plumb's set designs were brilliant. The 'home base' set had a staircase which appeared to be totally unsupported.

Petula Clark sings *Every Time we say Goodbye* to open part two of the show. My favourite version of this song ever. To get a boom in for all the live singing without upsetting Jimmy Boyer's marvellous lighting, minimum orchestra foldback was sent to the floor. None of the artistes ever complained, they just got on with it. Take note, Enge and Des!

One item called for a stripper sequence (Debbie Ryan from Raymond's Revue Bar.). After the strip, Petula implores her to consider that she is being exploited and whilst singing '*Pick Yourself Up*' Jon cleverly reversed the strip video-wise, so that Debbie finished up fully dressed. During the shooting of this sequence, the floor (and control rooms) mysteriously filled up with management of the male gender.

With Petula singing live, I would normally have her voice tracked enabling mixing later with more finesse with the level being kept down to avoid over modulation. My tape operator (he shall remain nameless) 'forgot' to plug this vital tracking claiming he was momentarily distracted! Thus, the voice level was a fraction lower than I would have intended and the mix to VTR had to be used on the final product. Guess what musical item they chose for that year's *Golden Rose Awards* entry?

My listing the crewing in detail points the choice of this show as my favourite UK program and my favourite Jon (classy at all times) Scoffield production. I have an off-air copy (1975) still fresh and entertaining apart from the corny (but interesting) commercials in the breaks.
Some ten years later, while having lunch with the lovely Chris Gage, the director of *Treasure Hunt* at Limehouse Television in Canary Wharf, writer Alma Cullen joined us and at one point I reminded her of *Traces of Love* (which she had written). She surprised me by stating that the interpretation of the show (by Jon Scoffield) was, in her opinion, appalling. She appeared almost venomous, almost blaming me. I think I put her clean off her lunch.

Another Jon Scoffield Special was *Dizzy Feet*. A mixture of all types of dancing from ballet to tap dance. Without dialogue this show highlighted multiple talents topped by Wayne Sleep performing a startling dance sequence lasting some five minutes in one take. Breathtaking Wayne at his best. This programme won the Golden Rose that year.

After the Muppet Shows finished in 1981, we did a series called *Starburst* directed by David C. Hillier (now living in Florida). The stars were always of the highest quality. I recollect a young Michael Barrymore fresh over from Australia doing his comedy routine whilst standing on his head (a challenge for any boom operator).

Starburst was the last light entertainment series to come out of Elstree before the closure. The last show featured Gene Pitney. Starburst was directed by David Hiller and choreographed by Nigel Lythgoe who later went to live in the States where he was enormously successful (American Idol etc). For his services in Great Britain he was awarded the OBE. Nigel; was in the control room while we dubbed the show. I have a Design & Maintenance fault report docket from 1984 written and signed by Nigel, it said;

> During a post-production dub, Ted Scott was complimentary to my choreographed item
> *'Something's Cookin' in the Kitchen'*
> THIS FAULT MUST BE RECTIFIED IMMEDIATELY.
> Signed. Nigel Lythgoe – choreographer.

I got severely hauled over the coals by the Head of Sound for allowing frivolous usage of a design and maintenance report book. For months, the maintenance guys gave me many suspicious looks.

On one *Starburst* I was called in the following day because Rita Coolidge was unhappy with the band sound and wanted it remixed. We got the multi-track out and she listened to every track and requested I drop the brass, the reeds and most of the strings. It seemed a bit empty to me, but she left delighted. Always keep the talent happy!

During 1982 the amount of productions was beginning to drop off. The writing was on the wall. Elstree ATV Studios were doomed to extinction. It had been ordained from 'them above' that a television production company had to reside in the area it served.

Years before, at a celebratory lunch in the ITCA building

for the successful first year world sales of The Muppet Show, I was introduced to a certain 'Lady X' who on being told my job remarked;

'Oh how fascinating, do you make those 'clippity cloppity' sounds with coconut shells?'

Great minds such as that compelled nearly a thousand people to relocate to Nottingham where a new studio was being built. We were all given the option to relocate, all expenses paid. I well remember one gentleman having quite a fight to claim for the removal of several dozen garden gnomes from his emporium in Boreham Wood to his new abode in Nottingham. Did they survived the inclement weather associated with that neck of the woods?

Having gone through the ATV years from my perspective (and a much potted version it is) it occurs to me that I have ignored so many productions. From the three outside broadcast and four studio crews operating at Elstree I have concentrated on only one, crew 4. The other crews could write up their experiences and fill these pages probably many times over.

Even considering crew 4's output, I haven't touched on *George & the Dragon* with the hilarious pairing of Sid James and Peggy Mount, the boom operators dream team. This was my first comedy series as a crew chief, it couldn't get much better. Peggy, despite her booming voice on camera, was a quiet lady, often knitting in outside rehearsal while Sid had his nose perpetually stuck in the *Racing Times.*

Arms dealer HINE played by Barrie Ingham had the boom operators nightmare throughout the series, a quiet actor in the back of shot with a very loud actor foreground. Barrie was appearing nightly at The Old Vic in two different Shakespeare roles aside from his Hine weekly turn round drama series. He never fluffed his lines and always appeared to be calmly reading a newspaper in outside rehearsal.

At Stratford-on-Avon, I saw Barrie in *Measure for*

Measure. He was fantastic. Health and safety these days would not have permitted some of the stunts he got up to. Barrie later immigrated to Los Angeles where he became voice-over king on television commercials.

The TENNESSEE ERNIE FORD Special featuring London hot spots was made for the American market. On a mock-up bus, he sang a medley from HMS Pinafore with much gusto. I never remember him not smiling.

Two big UK programmes produced and directed by Jon Scoffield were *'Bud n' Ches'* and *'One Man's Lauder* where Jimmy Logan impersonated Sir Harry Lauder who was a massive star in his time. Apparently he owned a mansion on the edge of Loch Lomond, which he designated *his* swimming pool! Jimmy took on the Lauder part with utter conviction. This was obviously something he wanted fervently to do. Heather, Jimmy Logan's PA, married Jon Scoffield shortly after the end of this production.

For *Bud n'Ches* Leslie Crowther did a terrific Chesney Allen, losing a couple of stone, whilst Bernie Winters put on weight to impersonate Bud Flanagan. They mastered the singing voices to an uncanny degree. They both practically lived the part and at one point Bernie Winters, singing *Any Umbrellas* broke down on camera. Jon Scoffield kept this in the final cut. Our present day television viewing would benefit from a re-run of both these shows.

    The six TOM JONES SHOWS I was lucky enough to sound direct while Bill Nuttall was having a vacation were a delight for me after eighteen Engelbert Humperdinck shows. Tom was a walk in the park!

    The spoof spy game-show *Masterspy* series starring William Franklyn was devised and written by Ronnie Taylor. A chapter should have been devoted to the Norman Wisdom sit-coms and Leslie Crowther's hit multi-series *My Good Woman* again both written by

Ronnie Taylor who also devised an innovative drama series starring CILLA BLACK with six episodes of different stories cleverly woven into the same set. Ronnie's last series was *A Sharp Intake of Breath* featuring David Jason which only recently had a re-run on Independent television.

There was also the SANDLER & YOUNG series Two funny Canadians not known here but mega in Canada. We recorded these shows in studio D while the American director worked in a scanner parked in the alley outside.

The RED SKELTON Show probably not seen in the UK, laden as it was, with American gags. I well remember the crew waiting on the embankment, opposite the House of Parliament for Big Ben to strike 10.00am. This was required for the opening of the programme. Imagine doing that today, they'd reproduce that in seconds electronically. How times have changed? During this time, nurses from the adjacent hospital leant out of windows to watch. Mr Skelton's ribald comments to them would not have been transmittable in Children's Hour.

I have hardly touched upon the *Thriller* series which ran for years. I did one episode which was shot entirely in the ATV Elstree offices at night. No sets were needed. Just empty corridors, mood lighting, and a sense of doom as a murderer sought his victim. All accompanied by Laurie Johnson's haunting music. This was always recorded on the floor of studio C with the dock doors open because Laurie could not work unless he could see daylight. Laurie did stacks of film series at the Elstree film studios. This classic and many other one-off dramas plus a cacophony of ad mags, soaps, a series for the disabled and children's programmes poured out of the studio with almost monotonous regularity - but it all came to an untimely end.

The ATV studios provided a platform for bigger things for a number of its staff. Notably;

Martin Campbell. A camera tracker who became a top-notch film director. His *Casino Royale* is my favourite all-time Bond film. The previous Bond film, Pierce Brosnan's last effort, was also directed by Martin and another cracker. Martin came to Britain from New Zealand.

Brian Truemay. From assistant floor manager to the founder of Bentley Productions responsible for *Midsomer Murders* and executive producer for Alamo Productions (Birds, Good night Sweetheart etc).

Tim Watson. Sound assistant to freelance director.

John Segal. Sound assistant to sound director at Sydney TV channel.

John Clark. Son of Nobby Clark, the ATV music fixer. John left the sound department to start up a business importing furniture from Italy.

Doug Hopkins. Sound assistant to heading production facilities house.

Andy Wernham. Sound trainee to Sound Director at LWT and successful freelance sound director. Andy had the dubious honour of sound directing the *Last Leg* series on Channel 4 – being the last ever programme to emanate from the iconic London Weekend Studios overlooking the River Thames (March 2018) before it transforms into expensive apartments. Another nail in the coffin of the big studios.

Martyn Gillman. Sound assistant to forming his own sound production company in Kuala Lumphur. Martyn went for a year to assist in opening a TV studio, stayed and married a local lass. I visited KL in 2018 and met Martyn and Geeta for a super lunch in the huge Mall.

Martin Baker. Assistant floor manager to executive position for the Jim Henson Organization. Apart from the

Muppet Shows, Martin was involved in all the Muppet movies over the years.

Peter Lodge. Long standing ATV sound director left to run his successful film production company in London.

Guy Caplin. Our very clever technical boffin actually designed the foldback speaker I have rambled on about so much. Guy now owns a Corporate video and training company.

David Millard. From Radio Luxembourg to sound assistant at ATV, leaving to become successful news director and later a hectic freelance life with stories galore, usually told over a hilarious, lengthy lunch.

Richard Holloway. Floor manager to executive producer for *The X Factor* and much more. ATV's 'golden boy' floor manager, a light entertainment specialist, always destined for the big-time.

Michael Gore. From sound assistant to head of sound at HTV Television. Later enjoying the ups and downs of the freelance world.

Brian Grant. From cameraman to film/TV director. Both he and **Tony Swain** became successful producers/directors when Elstree closed. Brian was responsible for multiple editions of *Video killed the radio stars.* I remember Brian quietly sitting on the rostrum by Ronnie Verrell, the Parnell orchestra star drummer. An experience that I also sampled a couple of times. Ronnie was a fascinating drummer to watch.

Paul Knight; Floor manager to executive producer of an independent film company (Black Beauty etc).

Roger Wilkinson; My number two for many years. Roger went To TV-AM as a sound director. Later, SKY got his services as a production manager where he travelled the world arranging technical details for future sporting fixtures. These days, Roger is still 'at it' recording and cohorting with local rock groups.

Geoff Sax; From floor manager to extremely successful film and television director world-wide, including STORMBREAKER in the Alex Ryder series.

Prior to closure, a massive party was organized in Studio C. Jack Parnell's Orchestra played on stage while a variety of people gave speeches lamenting the demise of ATV Lester. The wine and cheese flowed until BILL WARD the ultimate (and fearful) ATV studio boss gave a moving speech that virtually brought the house down. Apart from some post production work, the famous ATV site was now defunct. Actually, nothing short of a tragedy.

I would later work for Bill Ward in Israel on an Easter Special (see the Freelance life). Henry Bird and Peter Wernham decided not to take the Nottingham shilling, whilst I decided to try my hand in the freelance world, perhaps movies? But first, we are off to Spain for a ten week holiday to wallow in the past and contemplate the murky future over muchos tapas and rich Rioja.

***

20. The freelance world.

BACK FROM SPAIN, BACK TO REALITY. Late 1983 and freelance work in the television industry is virtually verboten. None of the ITV companies are allowed to hire freelance technical staff, thanks to unionism at that time. The BBC had endless staff hanging on hooks waiting for a chance to show their mettle. I had fired off a few letters but no response. Wait a minute though, didn't Lew Grade promise to set me up in films?

It's the wrap party for the Liberace series at Madam Tussauds - I had given my notice in a couple of weeks previous with the intention of getting into film sound. Having registered a company (*Sound on Film*) and budgeted some equipment I was raring to go. The Liberace wrap party is going swell and I see ATV executive Leslie Abbott talking to Lew Grade and nodding in my direction. Lew crosses over, puts his arm around my shoulders;

'I hear you're planning to leave us Ted?'

'Yes sir, I thought I'd try my luck in the film world'

'You want to be in films – you come and see me, I AM FILMS.'

His cigar is precariously close to my tie and the smoke is stinging my eyes.

'Thank you sir' is all I can muster.

'However' he continues with lowered voice; *'The business at the moment is not good, when the time is ripe we'll see what we can do. In the meantime we'll look after you, who is your head of department?'*

He got to me at the right time. I was having a twinge of cold feet. It had lately occurred to me that working in films didn't give total control of the sound output. On a TV Special, or sit-com, or whatever, the sound director is responsible for the final product, warts and all. In films, you may be a sound recordist where your location stuff is passed onto a sound editor. Or, a dubbing assistant finding sound effects; or, a final dub sound mixer at the behest of the film director in a dubbing suite.

This theory is surpassed in modern times. The term *Sound Designer* can cover all of the above and still keep it in your domain. This title is now common on a lot of expensively made series. Regretfully, it didn't really exist when I had visions of working in films.

Later that week, I am summoned to the office of Dickie Bonafaux (Head of sound and cameras) and asked to reconsider my resignation for a monetary consideration. I get a £1500 a year rise and a rocket from the union for having the gall to negotiate a contract without their permission. Called before union rep, cameraman Larry Dyer, I am nearly drummed out of the union.

Years later, before driving to Spain, I had fired off a letter to Lord Grade. I get a response eventually, *'Lord Grade regrets that at this time . . .'* etc. Well, let's not blame Lew; it was nearly ten years later.

***

21. Limehouse Television – Canary Wharf.

LUCKILY, I HAD SENT my CV to a new facility, Limehouse Television, situated on the Isle of Dogs. This innovative building was built on the site of a rum and banana warehouse on Canary Wharf.

Within days of my coming home, Head of Sound Ron Payne rang and booked me to do a sit-com the following week. The concept is two girls in an East End high rise, quite a nice show; not unlike Birds of a Feather. Director John Kaye Cooper had left LWT and I am hired for the series.

This is immediately followed by a drama series *Winter Sunlight* then another sit-com series *Relative Strangers* with Matthew Kelly. The months go by and I am working in Limehouse on a regular basis. Lady Luck has smiled on me again after that V2 rocket. I have fallen on my feet.

The Isle of Dogs was a controversial area in those days. Derelict warehouses were being converted into luxury apartments which the locals could not afford. The railway bridge over the entrance carried the threatening graffiti 'Kill a yuppie a day'. I was no yuppie but kept the car doors firmly locked.

Limehouse Studios was high tech and a joy to work at. The atmosphere there was terrific. Unionism has faded into the background and the camera department, largely from BBC and LWT, was of the highest professional standard.

Margaret Thatcher topped the bill at the opening of the studios where a couple of hundred people had gathered. The catering was supervised by Lorna who owned the floating restaurant moored outside the complex.

Gloria (the receptionist with the 'mostest') supervised just about everything else from her station in the luxurious reception area. Seemingly constantly on duty, Gloria epitomised the friendly structure of the entire Limehouse organization. Lines of demarcation were blurred and everybody seemed to muck in to help everybody else; the 'one big happy family' concept was very much in evidence. Many years later, Gloria is still waving the flag for Limehouse. Her Facebook page is a daily read for many.

In 2009 I celebrated a milestone birthday bash and invited friends and family to Lorna's boat, still moored in Canary Wharf. Lorna did me proud and I was chuffed to invite Gloria and her husband to share the moment. Gloria got to know a lot of my family.

Working there consistently for over eighteen months I had the pleasure of sound directing some wonderful shows. EMMA THOMSON did a special and we could see her talent was easily going to exceed the confines of a television screen.

DEREK JACOBI starred in a lavish version of *Cyrano de Bergerac*, which was shot on video and edited on film before re-transfer to video for the sound dub; a complicated process that offered three lots of time-code read-out virtually covering the picture when viewing for sound dubbing. The dub went on until 4:00 am and director Michael Simpson would have gone on for longer nit-picking the final battle sequence had I not got other plans; *'Sorry Michael, I've got an 11am date with a big white bird at Heathrow'*.

A classy MICHEL LEGRAND concert at the Festival Hall starred Stephan Grappelli and Nancy Wilson with a sixty-piece orchestra. We recorded the sound digitally (a first for me) and re-mixed in one of the two super

Limehouse sound control rooms. This Special was directed by David G. Hillier (ATV Starburst shows).

It was obvious that Limehouse was luring the cream of the directorial freelance world. The Spitting Image team had their puppet factory on site and recorded many shows there. Then, look what happened? Despite Gloria's ever demanding presence, it got bull-dozed to make way for the massive structure still known as Canary Wharf. It seemed inconceivable at the time that a beautiful studio complex could be zilched for a financial workplace. But someone, somewhere had the vision for the future. The site, which was bought and sold for millions, is now valued in billions.

Long before that I was offered a staff job, which I reluctantly turned down (I was making more dosh freelance than I ever earned at ATV) so they hired David Taylor, also from LWT, who took over my turf. I still got work, though not as frequent.

Treasure Hunt came my way for three series. Limehouse was the nerve centre for the roaming helicopters seeking clues for the studio bound contestants. We only ever saw Anneka Rice once during the entire run when the prize location would be London's Docklands.

Also, a lengthy stint on *The Business Daily* programme for Channel Four emanating from Canary Wharf and later from the Trocadero complex in Piccadilly. The Business Daily went out live at 5:30 am with various transmissions and pre-recorded inserts throughout the morning until the main (un-rehearsed) half hour transmission at midday.

For months, I parked at the Windmill Street National car park (£25 a day) before walking to the Trocadero, passing people coming out from various gaming clubs to be ready for that 5am report coming down the line from Tokyo or wherever. The car park attendant whinged to me on many occasions that I paid more in parking per week than he earned. Yeah, okay mate, but I wasn't sitting in a booth all day reading the *Daily Mirror*.

Often, for the main thirty minute midday slot, I sat at the sound desk looking at the floor through monitors. Three minutes to live transmission and *not a soul* to be seen? Had they forgotten? No, two minutes to go and journalists drifted onto the floor. Waiting cameramen pushed their monsters into position. Personal microphones were quietly fitted. One minute later and a floor manager appeared. Next door to sound control, the director and production assistant sat down with the vision mixer. Fifteen seconds and the FM called for quiet. The PA calmly counted down and off we went. Hectic at first, but eventually you got used to it. Often we did talking heads in the afternoon for tomorrow's transmission. Several days a week we never wrapped until 5pm. Add an hour or two travelling, they were long days. That car park attendant was never there when I left.

The outside recordings of *The Business Daily* were much more fun. With the terrific Limehouse camera team we dashed about the City of London recording business stuff which was invariably biked back for the midday transmission. If we had time, we grabbed a bite on the road.
 Once, in a City pub, we scoffed down a quick burger before returning to our vehicle to find the cameraman had left the camera (£20,000's worth) in the pub. It was retrieved and no, I'm not naming the cameraman.
 One cameraman I AM going to name is Colin Brewer. I did many dashes about the city with young Colin. He was very innovative, destined for bigger things with his use of krazy camera angles, which I'm sure started a trend. Apparently, Colin later changed his name to Happy! I wasn't surprised.
 Some finance centres had a land-line to Limehouse obviating the need for a bike but the plugging meant that often there would only be seconds to go before needed.
 I well remember an insert at the Daily Mirror with Robert Maxwell. The reporter, who would conduct the

interview, was late and Mr Maxwell was getting irate. Not the sort of gentleman who liked to be kept waiting. When the journalist finally arrived he explained that he had been delayed because of a fire in Fleet Street. Bob exploded and got on the phone to his news editor;
'There's a ****** fire on my doorstep and I'm the last to know it?'

That finance reporter was Dermot Murnaghan, now safely embedded at Sky News. The reporters on *The Business Daily* were all well-educated guys and girls with a massive grasp of the finance world. They travelled with us often in the truck working out their complicated questions en route. If there was time, a hostelry might be visited. Dermot happily discovered a watering hole that offered genuine Guinness from the barrel.

Another reporter, Hugh Pym (now BBC) was miles over six feet tall and he always had to bend at the knees when doing a piece to camera. When another reporter Greg Wood started his first day, we were having a quick lunch in St. Katherine's Dock when I got a call to say I was now a Grandfather. Greg did a lot of American reporting for the BBC. Every time I saw him, I remembered that day.

The Limehouse sound crew was headed by Ron Payne with Roy Drysdale. They were both from Southern Television and were the natural choice to be lured by the ex-STV directors who had just lost their franchise (remember Jimmy Gatward?). The Limehouse dream was their creation. Other sound crew members included Chris Blake and Dave Chapman. They had both previously run a sound mobile truck (owned by Richard Branson). I had worked with them before on the *No Excuses* series at ATV when we recorded on location.

Steve Blincoe also ex-STV was a bona fide boom operator, now a firmly established sound recordist in the freelance world. Judy Headman and Alex Rutherford were the other sound assistants. Judy is now an experienced sound recordist working in both the film and television word. Judy rang me recently and said she was having breakfast with Kelsey Grammar (Dr Frasier Crane) in Africa. I told her to tell him I nearly sued when I once fell off an armchair and damaged my arm while laughing at an episode of *Frasier*.

Both Ron Payne and Roy Drysdale had immense opera experience from their STV Glyndebourne days and they continued in this vein at Canary Wharf. On one opera I tracked two booms (first time for years, but that's the freelance business for you) during a ninety minute non-stop transmission. A huge orchestra, in one studio, was relayed (sound and picture) to the other studio with the conductor on separate picture monitors for the performers to follow.

After Limehouse died, Chris Blake and Dave Chapman formed their own sound production company *Audio Facilities Ltd*. The Limehouse experience for me was as close to ATV as I could possibly have got, great equipment, great crews and great shows. Not all big flag wavers, a mixture of kid's things, cooking and corporate stuff; you name it - but it had more than tied me over after the demise of ATV.

Called in to do a simple chat show between two people, I discovered the studio was packed jam tight with forty musicians. This youth orchestra was what the discussion was about. Undaunted and having no crew for this 'simple' show, I swung two booms over the ensemble and everybody was happy. I fondly member one cooking programme had Keith Floyd judging the 'best pie' competition. He proclaim they were all bloody rubbish. Well, what did they expect from Keith?

***

22. Bob Hope – lost in space

IN 1985 I WAS HIRED to sound direct the *Bob Hope's Eightieth Birthday Special* at the Lyric Theatre in Shaftsbury Avenue. The event would also be a fund raiser for Prince Phillip's World Wildlife Fund. Gary Smith and Dwight Hemion would produce the show. Dwight would direct from a temporary set-up under the stage whilst I would be in the Rolling Stones sound truck outside the stage door.
    Because of the complexity of the rig I had an extra 18-channel sound desk under my feet. As usual, everything was going to multi-track but I still did an on-line mix. Rather than sit back and check that all the microphones were peaking correctly, I could not but help mixing the programme as if it was going out live.
    The orchestra, under the direction of Alan Ferguson, was squeezed into the back stage wings on the proscenium arch side, a situation they vehemently (and uselessly) complained to me about. My sound crew was a mix of stage technicians and two freelancers I had never met before.
    One musical item with the band *Duran Duran* was pre-recorded at 10:30 pm the night before the show proper. During this recording Bob Hope, having checked into his hotel that day, arrived at the stage door only to be turned away by the stage door keeper, who, apparently never recognized him! Happily, Mr. Hope found this very funny.

On the night, the show was not far short of chaotic. Charlton Heston was starring in *The Caine Mutiny* in a nearby theatre. Because his show overran he had to rush to our theatre, still made-up and in the rain to do something with boxer Marvin Hagler - I know not what!

A couple of artistes failed to show and quick rescheduling was necessary. Ventriloquist Ray Allen with his puppet Lord Charles extended his act and Bernadette Peters performed a terrific song and dance number with a radio microphone stuffed down her low-cut dress. I kept fingers crossed that the mic wouldn't fall out as, unknown to anybody being no rehearsal, she was thrown from side to side by dancers.

Film star Debbie Reynolds was 'under the weather' or on some medication, as her vocal performance was marred. Never mind, said Dwight, over talk-back, we'll re-voice her in the States.

Patrick Allen, the voice-over king, had previously pre-recorded all the introductory announcements which were played in on the night.

Towards the end of the evening, one of my sound people had given a radio microphone kit to Prince Phillip's Equerry as the Duke was to appear on stage with Bob Hope receiving the World Wildlife Fund cheque. Ordinary human beings were not allowed near the Duke, so the sound guy explained to the Equerry how to connect it before leaving the royal box. This was hours before it would be needed, it couldn't be left pugged in otherwise the battery would have expired.

When the Duke arrived on stage, I faded up his microphone and got shush! Despite careful tutorage, the Equerry had not plugged the microphone into the transmitter. His excuse was that the vital connecting cable had not been presented to him. Dwight was convinced that I could fix this later, sorry about that Dwight. I did recommended Mike Yarwood who would have done Prince Phillip convincingly. Several days later, I got a small package from the Palace containing the vital connecting cable without explanation.

Bob Hope's monologue to the audience was marred because he was not able to see the cue cards. After the show finished and when the audience had gone, Gary Smith mustered up all the crew and stage people (anybody he could find) to sit in the first few rows of the stalls while Bob re-did his monologue on camera to bigger cue cards.

After the arduous and lengthy performance and the usual green room glass of vino, five sixteen-track audio tapes were handed over from the sound truck to production manager Billy Glaze who immediately took them to Heathrow for shipping to Los Angeles.

Two days later, I get a phone call at home.

'Hi Ted, this is Rod in LA, I'm still waiting for the sound tapes'

'What sound tapes?'

'For Bob Hope's eightieth birthday bash, we can't proceed without them'

I explain that I have no jurisdiction over the sound tapes once the show is over. Rod is distraught however and still thinks I've got them, holding them to ransom perhaps? Dwight is sitting in an LA editing suite twiddling his thumbs and wanting to re-voice Debbie Reynolds by dumping her original vocal performance and using the band tracks on the multi-track tapes.

Dwight had not used a vision mixer to cut the show as it was progressing. Instead, he had isolated all the camera outputs to separate recording machines and was now faced with a massive edit job. Juggling the items around meant that Patrick Allen's intros were often wrong, i.e., *'And now, here is Bernadette Peters'* had to be replaced by *'. . And that was Bernadette Peters'*. Patrick had to redo most of his tracks.

The missing sound tapes were eventually traced to New York via Pan Am – then never to be seen again.

Were they lying in a remote customs shed in Alaska or Bali? Dwight had to go along with my on-line mix. From a sound balance point of view it was quite transmittable, obviously nothing could be done voice replacement-wise and nor could the sound be re-laid to avoid generation problems. They were stuck with what they had.

The show went out coast-to-coast the following night. A coast-to-coast transmission involved all the station affiliates to record the show for later transmission at their local times. After multi-editing by Dwight and safety copying, this meant that the show went out with something like eighth generation sound – rather hissy, I imagine?
But, what if a decent on-line mix hadn't been available? Verging on a disaster, that's what! Instead it was readily available on the master videotapes.

Modern sound desks today are capable of memorising a rehearsal mix and duplicating it later automatically. Thus, the trend has been to set up your levels, ensure the correctness of the sound you require and sit back and do nothing but watch the faders move all by themselves. As if by magic.

Had I possessed that facility and used that method, poor old Dwight Hemion would have twelve 2" videotapes with the sound tracks full of . . . nothing. Just audio pixels. As it happens I could no more sit there watching the faders magically move, I would have intervened. Hence the on-line mix.

***

23. Paul Daniels to Birds of a Feather

FAMOUS PHOTOGRAPHER KEITH EWART had invested in a television facility in Wandsworth. Ewarts was a popular venue and I did many, many productions there. Lots of Muppet Show stuff re-edited by Peter Harris for VHS sales brought back old Muppet memories as we re-worked the songs and sketches.

A PAUL DANIELS series was fascinating, if only because Paul worked without shoes on and liked everybody else to do the same. I saw his stage show in London and still think he was one of the best visual comedic/magic performers ever. A two hour show, just him, the lovely Debbie McGee and the audience. Recently she has built up quite a reputation by appearing and nearly winning *Strictly Come Dancing* after the sudden and untimely death of Paul.

An interesting Ewarts contract for me was AFTER DARK. This involved a live chat show from midnight onwards with a mixture of guests who sat round a table laden with food and drink. Cameras were out of sight behind gauze and producer Sebastian Scott requested that the guests were not to be mike'd up in case they wanted to leave suddenly (which they sometimes did!) and that no microphones should be seen in shot as this would spoil the illusion of an informal get together.

Always willing to experiment, I placed several small microphones under the ledge of the table held adjacent to where the guests would sit using lots of camera tape encased in rubber. There was invariably a bowl of fruit on the table and I hid a microphone in there as well. Of course, there was no rehearsal as the guests often arrived five minutes before transmission and occasionally later.

It was all a bit hit and miss. Some guests had no voice, others yelled. The surfeit of alcohol didn't help and glasses suddenly banging down on a table with six hidden microphones could have certainly have stopped any viewers nodding off. To keep us alert in the early hours, Keith often popped into the sound control room with his parrot to have a chat. Him, me and the parrot! There was no set off-air time, it conversation flagged or the guests appeared to have consumed more than enough liquor, Sebastian would declare a wrap. It was innovative stuff but audio-wise, not a resounding success.

One memorable day occurred when I was contacted in the morning by a production company to operate a boom that very late afternoon in the Molinaire Studios off Piccadilly. It was to be a live election programme. On arrival the director, a politically inclined young gentleman, who had never seen a boom before, was concerned that I would keep getting in shot while covering the questions from the audience of sixty or so, 'don't knows' who would be questioning a panel of well-known politicians. My boom had a television monitor and I was able to dip in and out without being seen. Money for old rope. After a short mock rehearsal, the director was so impressed that he insisted I get a credit on the end roller. This was extremely unusual; boom operators should be heard but never 'seen' (on the roller).

After the transmission, I arrived at Ewarts for the *After Dark* rig. Keith had obviously watched the pre-election broadcast (Molinaire being a rival production house) and had noticed my sound credit. He and his parrot passed me in reception; *'Busy day, Ted?'* he enquired with a knowing smile.

You bet Keith. I hadn't finished my busy day by a long chalk. After Dark came off air at 3:30 am. I drove to Docklands, where after a few hours kip in the car I was ready for an early morning recording of *Treasure Hunt* coming from Australia (hence the time slip).

On *Treasure Hunt* we never got the visual output of Anneka Rice's end of the show, just audio. This was relayed to the floor via earpieces for Kenneth Kendall, Wincey Willis and the contestants. It was imperative that the contestants never heard the pre-show chat between the director and Anneka otherwise they would know the location for which they would strive nearly an hour for – end of show. Director Chris Gage would not have forgiven me for that.

Another nice contract was *The Ticket*. This was a programme for Television South visiting all the theatres in the south of England. Martin Hawkins both lit and operated the camera. We recorded inserts of many provincial stage productions on tour.

Wayne Sleep gave a very serious interview on the ballet scene in Hastings! Peter McEnery, the star of our *Clayhanger* series at ATV, was surprised when I turned up for an interview at a theatre with a boom pole, a sound mixer strapped around my neck and heavily garbed in Berber as I helped Martin Hawkins hump in his camera gear and lighting equipment.

The charming Michael Aspel 'compelled' us to sample his latest batch of claret, making us late for an interview with Ronnie Corbett in a Soho upstairs restaurant. During this, I had to stop the recording as I was picking up taxis on the radio mike. Shortly after, Martin stopped the recording again because he ran out of battery power for the camera. Mr. Corbett was very unimpressed; *'This sort of thing never happens at the BBC'* he snorted.

Again another pleasant freelance venue for me was CTVC at Bushey, Herts. The studios in lush grounds were conceived by J. Arthur Rank as a religious teaching centre. Now it was doing more commercial productions which included a long running children's series.

The sound department was run by Harry Jacobs and John Parker (both ex-ATV). I did a 'fish-pole' for John at Ford Open Prison amidst a bunch of 'hardened' criminals who were living in conditions that both John and I would not have complained at. A super restaurant and well equipped gym made life quite good for the in-mates.

At CTVC I was assigned to work with seven bishops who were learning the 'tricks' of appearing comfortable on telly, or radio broadcasts where telephone etiquette was important. I had to mock introduce a caller (another Bishop) and liaise between them on the telephone. Those that know me will ponder how I was chosen for this task?

William G. Stewart hired me to 'sound design' a non-transmittable pilot of a show called *Fifteen To One*. I pointed out that fifteen microphones offered the possibility of a late fade, or two. To obviate that, I devised a system where all the microphones were recorded before the fader, so a late fade of a contestant could be found and reinserted later. I understand the facility was often used by the sound guys at Ewarts. The sound crew there always went unrecognised on the roller. Unfairly I think just because they were 'merely' a facilities house. They contributed stacks of programmes for the networks.

Being booked for a series where the sound technical requirements called for seven radio microphones got me wondering. Could be a chat show I thought? No, it turned out to be *Drop the Dead Donkey*. Recorded at break neck speed, my little army of good boom operators were a godsend. The production team was a nervous bunch; the technical run raced along disregarding technical queries because that would interfere with the artiste's concentration. (Psst! Outside rehearsals are designed for actors. A technical run was to sort out technical problems).

I never did discover who thought the show could be done on seven radio mikes. We used to play taped music as the audience were being seated. Producer Andy Hamilton asked me if I could cut out the gaps between tracks as the momentary silence might cause the audience to get restless. Always keep the talent happy – but cut the gaps out? Come on, Andy . . .

An equipment hire facility (ESP) got me the *Birds of a Feather* gig. The pilot for Alomo Productions was made at the Elstree Film Studios, a four wall studio. This entails all equipment having to be temporarily wheeled in for the show, a nightmare scenario for everyone.

For the pilot, the director Nic Phillips, vision mixer Moyra Bird and producer's assistant Bernadette Darnell, sat in the back of a small van watching several TV monitors a few feet away overseen by facilities owner Derek Oliver with a perpetual soldering iron at the ready for trouble shooting. BBC trained, Bernadette was another of the old school PA's capable of doing three things at once. These days, you don't get many of them to the pound! I was ensconced in the driver's cab on a reversed passenger seat with a portable sound mixer virtually on my lap. I wore headphones to mix as the constant chat from the team just in front of me and the whine of two VTR machines were very off-putting.

Later, we moved into rooms above the studio floor. The studio was large enough for several sets and an audience area. The sound equipment supplied by ESP was not what I was used to and neither was their crewing which was often on a hit or miss basis.
Once, they provided a film boom operator who, on arrival at the studio told me he had never operated a studio boom, only a hand held 'fish-pole' – poor guy was terrified. Later, I managed to get good boom ops like Paul Botham,

John Parker, Ken Campbell, Michael Gore and Steve Lindsay whenever they were available.

From a sound perspective, all situation comedies require the services of experienced boom operators (Yes, I know I *keep* going on about this). Lighting directors like to go for optimum lighting and this usually means that booms have a problem catching sound without throwing boom shadows. In the end a compromise is found.

One dispute with a lighting director ended with him telling me we all had to compromise. I explained that 'compromise' was the sound department's middle name. I grabbed the boom and put it front of the actors mouth and said; *'That's perfect sound'* – pulling the mike two feet above his head I said; *That's a compromise'* then taking the mike ten feet away looking at the distant actors ear; *'That's **not** a compromise'* – he got the picture and we all got back to square one, happy (ish).

Some cameramen like to offer the director a shot without regard for the boom. My method to combat this was to ask the boom operator to get way out of shot. As the dialogue suddenly becomes far away the director gets the message and the shot is adjusted. Once more – compromise is the order of the day. Boom operators are still gold dust. What would Coronation Street do without them?

The Biko Inquest was shot at London's Riverside Studios in 1984. A star studded cast headed by Albert Finney with Richard Johnson, Michael Aldrich, Michael Davenport, Edward Hardwicke, Michael Gough and John Standing, all contributed to a stellar production directed by Graham Evans.

We operated from small truck outside the studio. I sat behind Graham and his PA Sonia Hampson. Boom operators, Paul Botham and John Martin worked with lighting director Jimmy Boyers and cameramen Stan Pilgrim, Roy Simper and Mike Whitcutt, all ex-ATV.

The edit and dub was at a TransVideo, a small facility in Ickenham and Albert Finney worked alongside me for a couple of days after VT editor Phil Moss (ex-ATV) had completed the edit for the ninety minute show. I recollect that we had an audience for a complete non-stop telling of the trial having already shot the entire programme for close-ups and a constructed shooting script. Richard Attenborough made a feature film of the Biko story. I like to think our version from Riverside stood up well against it.

Obviously, no audience reaction was required for that programme. Situation comedies are a different kettle of fish. Without an expensive sound dub with a laughter machine, it is imperative that good audience pick-up is achieved. On Birds of a Feather at Elstree, I used six audience microphones. Later, at Teddington Studios, I got up to eighteen. Writers Maurice Gran and Lawrence Marks would count the audience microphones to ensure I got the best pick-up; as if I would short-change them?

I am convinced that other sound crews around the world will confirm my belief that a sit-com is the most difficult type of show. It can be tricky with three or four booms to switch between, sound effects to run in and VT inserts to fade up. Plus a constant hand on the audience group fader, whilst carefully following the script and picture cutting.

A usual scenario is a scene, or portion of, has to be re-shot four times because the artistes have dried. On the fourth take they get through it but there is a boom shadow. The sound department get dirty looks and often accompanied by whispered oaths.

The average sitcom ensured that at the end of the day you will drive home whacked out. I well remember after an arduous *Goodnight Sweetheart* studio recording, walking to the car park with veteran cameraman Alan Beale (ex-ATV). It was approaching midnight, Woefully, Alan shook his head saying;

'I'm getting too old for this'

I replied; *'Alan, I'm **already** too old for this'*.

The *Birds of a Feather* girls Pauline Quirke, Linda Robson and Lesley Joseph were a joy to work with. Wherever we went on location, an audience would quickly gather and the girls would chat as if they were next door neighbours. With them, what you saw was what you got. Once at lunch on the catering bus, Linda asked my advice about buying a car (as if I knew?) she had just passed her driving test.

'How much have you got?' I enquired.

'Eight 'undred quid' she replied.

I pointed out she wouldn't get much for that. Bit different now eh Linda? The girls have been very successful and well deserved too. The weekly turn round of Birds was hard work for them. Often they went on the set without knowing their lines too well, but their good humour got them through every time. The audience may have spent longer at the studio than planned but they always went away with happy faces.

We did three terrific Christmas Specials. The first in Berlin shortly after the Wall came down, with director Nic Phillips. We saw fields of derelict Russian tanks as we filmed well into East Berlin. We saw young Russian soldiers willing to sell their fur hats as apparently they hadn't been paid for months. Probably could have bought their guns too!

The following year we went to Majorca, where we all had a ball. One sequence was on a beach at sunset. It was a massive hike getting the gear down a very steep incline. After we finished we all mucked in taking the gear back up again to the trucks. Yes, even the stars of the show!

The wrap party was held in a local restaurant and I well remember Peter Polycarpou (Pauline's show husband) standing up after the meal and singing us a beautiful love song in Greek. He later starred in *Phantom of the Opera*.

The third special was set in Los Angeles in the summer of 1993. Martin Hawkins was cameraman. The storyline was the girls discovering they have a long-lost relative who transpires to be a famous personage living in Hollywood. Writer Geoff Dean had Roger Moore in mind but he was 'unavailable' Then, Dudley Moore - also unavailable. Other names came, and went. Several days before we were due to start shooting, we flew out to find locations, organize equipment and crew. A small part was written for Richard Branson and he arranged upper class flights for us; both ways. Wow! That's the only way to travel (hardly been able to do so since).

Geoff Dean was hastily re-writing while production assistant Samantha Donavon was constantly revising the script. I believe that Mr Dean tried to give Sam some re-writes extremely late one night. She complied but said once more and I'm off home. The PA's revenge! Good for you Sam.

The part was eventually taken by George Hamilton, the sun-tanned, smiling American actor. Apparently, he knew the *Birds of a Feather'* show having seen it in England. Obviously perfect for the part. It was rumoured however that George had a short fuse and that it would be advisable to shoot his bits then let him go home while we filled in the blanks, rather like a feature film. In television shooting out of sequence often happens but never letting an artiste to do his bit in isolation then bugger off home.

The first sequence we shot was in a famous Hollywood restaurant on the Pacific Coast Highway. George would be discovered sitting at a table with a dozen or so extras until Leslie Joseph, passing by and noticing him reverts to the scripted dialogue. No words between George and the other people at his table were plotted. But I had hidden microphone in the middle of the table. Even if only to pick up sound effects.

When Mr. Hamilton came out of make-up, he was ushered to the table and I listened in. He immediately got into an animated conversation with the extras asking them what other productions they had worked on. It was soon obvious to me that George had a very long fuse and turned out to be the most charming man ever. He never bunked off early and took an avid interest in the storyline.

We shot sequences on the back lot of Universal Studios and I was able to wander around the massive *Back to the Future* set. The clock tower is still there. Then onto Rodeo Drive, where we were shooting in a famous dress store.

Being a Sunday, the store was closed. I saw a row of twenty, or so sequined gowns priced at $35,000 each. Yes, thirty five thousand . . . (that was a lot of money then!) that's Rodeo Drive for you. I pointed the dresses out to Linda, she said Marks and Sparks had similar for just a few quid.

A seedy motel on Sunset Blvd was also used where I was accosted several times by two drug dealers, both armed! We also did sequences in the beautiful *Mondrian Hotel* on Sunset Blvd, where we were all staying. If you ever get to stay there, request any room starting in seven . . . they are all corner suites. I got one all to myself while Pauline and Linda didn't. I pointed out the old maxim . . . Age before beauty!

They were long days but most enjoyable. Charlie Hanson decided to get married in LA and threw a wedding party on the hotel rooftop. The ceremony was a hoot with the incredible pastor (and his trio) singing *'It Had to Be You'* to the gorgeous bride and nervous groom. Pauline & Linda were bridesmaids and a jolly time was had by all.

After the wrap, George Hamilton had arranged a private room at a famous LA club (I think it was the *Viper Room*?) for all the crew where a sumptuous meal was laid on (probably blowing his fee). George was such a friendly person and while the rest of the young crew danced away to the loudest disco I have ever heard, George recounted to me the sad story of his son's drug habit.

We also shot a sequence in the garden of a gorgeous mansion in Beverly Hills. The fences were inundated with

Armed Response signs. George told us he had a pad like that once but chucked it up because it was costing $8000 a month just for security. Apparently, he then downgraded to a penthouse on Sunset. Bit of a comedown, George? No way. It would be the absolute height of luxury.

He regaled about the car crime in Hollywood. It seems they could steal a brand new Mercedes Coupe and have it totally broken down in ten minutes for parts. George drove a beautiful, dark green Rolls Bentley convertible. He said it was the only one in Hollywood and therefore un-nickable. George Hamilton – great guy.

Another sit-com project from Alomo called *Get Back* starred Ray Winstone, Larry Lamb and the indestructible John Bardon. He had only to walk onto a set when it would virtually light up. After recordings of this gritty comedy show I wheeled the booms into the adjacent Elstree film studio where I was doing Lenny Henry's *Chef* Sit-com series the very next day. *Chef* was shot with film cameras. Small TV cameras had to be strapped to their filmic brothers enabling the vision mixer to cut the pictures seen by the audience. This transpired to be a convoluted method of working.

The film cameras took ages to get from set to set, allowing the audience to lose concentration. One set had Lennie Henry in bed with his wife holding a very quiet conversation. The bed was on a wooden rostrum and any movement resulted in loud squeaking. I pointed this out to the director and he said it was a sound problem and not to bother him.

However, during the edit, it became *his* problem and he tried to contact me. Bit late old chap. I was in Norway doing *Casablanca*. Shooting a sit-com on film was not a walk in the park. Presumably, someone had seen the way the Americans do things (*Cheers, Frasier etc*). The trouble was, the Americans did it properly.

Later, I embarked on another Alomo Production series *The Old Boy Network.* This was a spy sit-com thriller directed by the legendary Sidney Lotterby and starring Tom Conti and John Standing. With masses of telephone distort sound effects and other visual tricks that stretched the facilities offered by a four wall-er, Sydney often requested a sound effect that had to be ordered and paid for. He was unable to comprehend this having left the comfort of the BBC and other well equipped ITV studios where Aladdin's Cave would be provided if requested. But, it was an unusual, well written show and would be well worth seeing again.

Robert Lindsay starred with David Threllfall and James Ellis in the weirdest ever crazy six part sit-com called *Nightingales*. They were night security guards. Actually, there were four guards but one had died (un-reported) three years earlier and the others shared his pay packet.

Their inventiveness and crazy antics enhanced the production enormously. I remember one show being cancelled at the outside rehearsal stage because the artistes didn't think the script was good enough. This brilliant 13-part series directed by Tony Dow is available on DVD.

Alomo also came up with a charming series called *Take the Floor* featuring ballroom dancing. Dance programmes were always popular. The BBC's original *Come Dancing* was the more traditional affair with the gentlemen dancing with number on their back.

Goodnight Sweetheart with Nicholas Lyndhurst was another Alomo winner. Nick had been a boy star in *Peter Pan* (ATV 1975) and he was delighted when I was able to provide him with a VHS of that show. I did sixteen '*Sweethearts*' before being replaced by a 'sweet' deal involving Teddington's own sound crew (i.e. they did it for less dosh). One episode called for a massive air raid sequence to be shot on a rooftop set.

I got to Teddington Studios at 6:00 am that morning to make up about twenty minutes of air raid sirens, bombs, gunfire and what have you. The lengthy sequence was shot in one take and at one point I was rolling three tape machines and several spot effect machines so the explosions coincided with the script. (There was no, *cue tape please, Ted*, from the production gallery, who seemed to think the sound effects all appearing in the right places was some sort of unexplained magic).

I think this was the episode where we re-shot several sequences after the audience had been dismissed and I went out to the car park around midnight and whinged en route to Alan Beale. This innovative series by Lo and Mo (Alomo) can still be seen on satellite telly.

They were a very prolific pair of writers coming up with many successful series. To have a couple of hits is extraordinary, to go beyond that – magic. I once reminded Lo and Mo about a series they wrote for ATV in the sixties called *Roots*. I think it concerned the world of dentistry? Directed by Keith Farthing, we shot a lot of it in Wales. I think only two or three of the six-part series ever got shown. My recollections fell on deaf ears!

***

24. Dallas to Israel via Bergen

In 1987 my ATV colleague, Mike Gore had now left the HTV Bristol studios and he got me involved in a trip to Dallas and Los Angeles where we would seek out and report on the new digital sound equipment made by Lexicon for a planned 'soap' that would go out all over Europe in different languages. The trip was organized by the Dutch Government.

The idea for the project was developed by British director Andrew Wilson, who would be heavily involved throughout. We found the digital desk on display at the massive Dallas Convention Centre but it had no innards, just a carcass and therefore unable to show off its supposed capabilities.

Onto LA where we met up with the Head of Sound honcho at Universal Studios, one David 'Doc' Goldstein. He was an incredibly knowledgeable guy – aged about twenty five! They were already into digital and I think we learned a lot. After LA, I flew to Boston to see the missing innards and get a demo of the desk from Lexicon's sales manager, Brian Zolner – another 25 years old whiz kid. Regretfully, the project came to nothing as Andrew Wilson tragically died of cancer the following year.

Later, I was able to repay Mike Gore by involving him in a series to be made in Norway. As a result of a call from the boss of Stageway Productions working for the newly formed Norwegian Channel 3, Ole Bjorn flew me to

Bergen to recce the location for a night club style light entertainment series to be called *Casablanca*.

Shooting would be in a large café/restaurant close to the waterfront. Ole further envisaged a twelve-piece 40s style band with girl singers in the Andrews Sisters mould. Only the vocal microphones would be seen and these would need to be in 40s style (we hid radio mics in the shell of microphones of the period).

All the orchestra microphones were hidden with reasonable success. We used small microphone pick-ups attached to the string instruments, a first for us, they were in their infancy. Took a long time to set up and not as successful as hearing a string section via the conventional method. These days they are extensively used and much improved.

It was further pointed out that a sing-along would occur as the Norwegian audiences liked to 'join in'. As previously mentioned (*Sing-a-long a-Max*) this requirement could prove tricky. It entailed placing a lot of hidden speakers and microphones throughout the café. Luckily, there were potted palms and shrubs galore in which we could hide the gear, often having to paint the cables green to camouflage them.

Apart from a small stock of sporting events sound equipment in their impressive new scanner which would be used later for the Winter Olympics in Lillehammer the production company had no other sound equipment and wanted me to buy it for them. I was very busy at that time with *Chef, Get Back* and *Birds of a Feather*. Mike Gore to the rescue he organized everything, purchasing the right gear at the right price for Stageway – I was pleased that Mike was available.

We went to Bergen, and did the pilot which went very well. An hour of continuous music and song. The dialogue was all in Norwegian. Awkward for judging audience reaction! No re-takes. The audience turned up in full evening dress, several in kilts! (Having paid for the privilege). Amazingly, the sing-song turned out to be a medley of British war-time songs; *The White Cliffs of Dover*, etc, and they knew every word. For the following nine shows, I flew backwards and forwards from Heathrow. Mike sometimes stayed and did a few of the shows himself. We split the fee and stayed in the gorgeous Admiral Hotel overlooking Bergen's fantastic waterway.

We had dinner one night with guest star Gilbert O'Sullivan, who had married a Norwegian girl. Eating out in Bergen was great but the wine was horrendously priced. One waterside café did roasted reindeer – marvellous. If you want a terrific weekend break, Bergen ticks all the boxes. It usually rains once a day but the inhabitants are the friendliest ever and the hotels have racks of umbrellas.

In the summer of 1987, Bill Ward (ex-ATV boss) asked me to go to Israel to work on an Easter Special for ITV called *'The Gospels.* It would feature Rick Wakeman's rock group and hosted by Robert Powell. On arrival, Bill picked us at the airport and on the manic drive back to Tel Aviv seafront he was sometimes half a microsecond late pulling away from the lights. Several manic drivers' waived fists and shouted insults at him as they flew by. I said to Simon French (the senior cameraman); *'Have they any conception who they are shouting at?'*

Bill Ward was a feared warlord at ATV often striking terror into the hearts of young directors. However, this was a calmed down Bill Ward; he enjoyed the shoot enormously. We did the show in Caesarea, a 2000 year old amphitheatre (reputed to be built by King Herod) overlooking the sea up the coast from Tel Aviv.

I had got Derek Oliver's ESP Company involved to provide the camera gear.

We had previously gone on a week's recce, returning a couple of weeks later for the two week shoot. Hiring sound equipment in Israel was tricky. There were so many things happening there, documentaries and what-have-you, gear was at a premium. We managed to get a tacky truck and once again I tracked everything and re-mixed in London.

The huge orchestra was mainly comprised of Russians. True to the tradition of the Musicians Union, they demanded, and got, world rates. For the opening shot the camera zoomed out from a dusky sun scene over the sea revealing the string section. As if on cue, two helicopter gun-ships flew into frame. Awesome. We all wonder whether Billy Glaze has organized it. Wouldn't put it past him. However, it did graphically pointed life in that neck of the woods.

After the concert, we travelled all round Israel to the various holy sites connected with the Gospels telling various video stories. Robert Powell was the anchor for the segments separate from the concert. En route to Jerusalem for the finale of the show where Jesus carrying the cross was re-enacted every month for the tourist trade, we are held up for half an hour by a procession of Israeli tanks on exercise. We could easily miss the event. Suddenly, a tank commander halts his machine and allows our small convoy of crew, artistes and equipment, to pass. Is that Billy Glaze again?

Two things stick in mind about Israel; it was rather warm! 47 degrees centigrade. In Turkey, people were dying of heat exhaustion. Here in Tel Aviv people were on the beach. The gentlemen in bathing trunks, the ladies in full Arab garb, not an inch of skin showing.

I discovered they have more churches than Canterbury has pubs. One church was built on the site of an older church which was built on the site of . . . you get the picture? We flew El Al and I was interrogated on both outward trips from Heathrow for twenty minutes by the same intelligence officer, a young girl who asked the same (very personal) questions - twice. Our stewardess en route told me that a fly couldn't get into Israel without being thoroughly checked. If it got that same intelligence officer girl, I believed her.

This production in Israel was high-lighted by the presence of BILLY GLAZE. He had worked with Bill Ward countless times and also the Muppet team.

Billy was a remarkable floor manager at ATV, he ruled the studio floor with an iron fist accompanied by a tongue in cheek grin. When Billy yelled *QUIET*...pins could be heard to drop.

One example; a music show is in rehearsal progress at Elstree. They are about to run out of dress rehearsal time. There is a sound problem. A microphone has gone down. It is a condensor microphone attached to a long thin stem with a detachable head, the cable runs to a power box. This box has a power cable to a wall point and a microphone cable also to that wall point. A fault can be any one of those combinations, or, worst-case-scenario, a double fault where a cable is replaced without solving the problem then switched back to the original cable. The director is frothing at the mouth and asks Billy Glaze to ascertain the problem.

Don Warren, a crew sound number two, is bending over the offending microphone amplification box trying to ascertain the fault. Billy Glaze approaches him for the third time, patience is running thin.

'How much longer sound?'
'Don't know Billy'
'Don't know? What the **** does that mean?'
'Means what it says Billy . . . don't know'
'What's the problem?'
'Shall I explain or get on with it?'
'Why not ******* get on with it **and** explain as well?'
'It's tricky'
'Why?'
'Cos it's technical, Billy'
'Technical bollocks – how much longer?'

I had a similar embarrassing situation on the ANN-MARGRET show. In rehearsal she appeared from make-up ready to sing a number on a plush sofa. We have a hand microphone ready for her and Dwight Hemion cues the pre-recorded orchestra track.

I cue tape, the orchestra starts, and I fade up the mic and . . . zilch. It isn't working.

It was working two minutes before. My sound guy on the floor changes the microphone – no luck. Changes the microphone cable – no luck. This cable is one of three to reach the wall point. All are changed - no luck. Changes the wall point to which the cable is attached – no luck.

This all takes at least ten minutes. Miss Margret is cool as a cucumber, very patient. Un-flappable Dwight Hemion has glanced at me a couple of times through the control room window. Then he raised an eyebrow. Is Dwight's patience showing signs of cracking?

Short of changing the sound guy I have one other option. Rig a new microphone with new cables into a new wall point. It works. Later, we discover the fault – is was a **double** fault. Two of the original elements had gone down.

Why? No idea. Microphones misbehave when being constantly moved around, rigged, then de-rigged they eventually suffer fatigue. It's usually cables. Forty microphones in the bandroom, for instance, never go down. They are static and happy.

Don Warren's search for the sound breakdown that Billy Glaze was so concerned about was also the result of a double fault. Wasn't too technical after all, Billy.

In Israel, Billy is first assistant director, floor manager, general liaison between the crew and the management (Bill Ward etc) and procurer of anything that might be required whether human or otherwise. .

The crew are of mixed race, to say the least. Billy has five assistants, all local, either Jewish or Arabs. They all idolise him. One sixteen year old Mustapha follows Billy everywhere with a folding chair in case the aged Billy wants to rest. Another carries iced water for him. Billy is garbed in khaki shorts well below the knee and a weather beaten khaki shirt and huge bush hat with tassels. He could be an extra in the *Raiders of the Lost Ark*.

At breakfast in the Arab owned hotel Billy gets two fried eggs with several rashers of bacon and brown toast every morning. Everybody else has the choice of boiled eggs (with a number pencilled on them indicating length of boil) and the obligatory cucumber salad. The star of the show sees Billy's fried eggs and plateful of juicy bacon and requests the same. No chance, boiled egg or cucumber or nothing.

Billy's presence and abilities on the location shoots are invaluable. Want a job done . . . get Billy Glaze. Language may be a bit ripe! On the flight home Billy is surrounded by *El Al* cabin crew plying him with drinks and goodies.

That's Billy Glaze.

***

25. The end is nigh . . .

HTV Bristol provided me with a lot of work, mainly floor assistant or doing grams on the local news show. Most of the inserts for the news were on film and therefore mute. Sometimes these inserts didn't appear until minutes before transmission. A running order gave you some idea to select a sound effect to suit the location. One insert was entitled 'Bristol Docks' I pulled out the cassettes for ships horns, cranes operating, etc., and 'on the night' when the insert was played in, I let loose with my barrage of sound. The first words of the voice over were; *'Bristol Docks are quiet today, as the strike continues . . . .'*

I slowly faded out everything and amazingly, no-one in production appeared to be bothered.

After one news job in Bristol, I wasn't required until 2:00 pm the next day so I decided to drive home for the night. It was the time Michael Fish said *'Hurricane? What hurricane?'* It took me five hours back and another five returning the following day avoiding fallen trees etc.

Head of sound, Michael Gore had a musical show at Bristol needing three freelancers. He got me, Bill Nuttall and Dave Langridge (ATV and TV/AM), a top heavy, motley collection of three ex-sound directors.

The brilliant ventriloquist Ray Charles 'asked' Lord Allen to make several funny comments about us on rehearsal. Ray had known us all at various venues throughout the years. Years before I gave Lord Charles a radio microphone pinned to his dinner suit as if he were a real person. Ray was amazed no-one had ever done this before.

Another enjoyable gig was *Desmond's.* A barber shop set enabled Desmond's friends and relative to meet and get involved in various escapades. We recorded this in front of an entirely black audience. No 'added laughter' dub need on this production. I did the first series with Martin Hawkins and directed by the brilliant Mandie Fletcher at the Limehouse Studios. Regretfully producer, Humphrey Barclay took the production to LWT, where Charlie Hanson took the reins. Andy Wernham, son of Peter Wernham (ATV's head of sound effects), did most of the following five series. Thus, Martin, Mandie and I lost that gig.

Between Alomo Production commitments, several shows at Fountain Studios came my way. *'Winjun Pom'* a puppet/animation/live artist show was very clever and inventive directed by Steve Bendelack of Spitting Image fame.

In 1993, film director John Henderson did a six-part comedy involving classrooms and school kids and dotty teachers. Called *Bonjour la Classe,* it starred Nigel Planer. Newcomer Martin Clunes appeared in a couple of the episodes. It was pretty obvious Martin was going far down the road to stardom. On one occasion, we covered a football match on the playing fields of the private school at Radlett in Hertfordshire. It had been raining and the pitch was very muddy.

The camera rushed around following the action, the hand-held boom was energetically following and I was connected to both via umbilical cords. At one point, the camera made a sudden move, Ian Coles, operating the pole followed sharply and their quick action pulled me over. This coincided with the football hitting me squarely in the face. I fell heavily in the mud but still protecting my portable mixer.

At this point John Henderson foresaw a replacement being needed for the rest of the week. No chance, John. In the freelance world, no show is no dough. After those shoot days, the meticulous boom operator, Ian Coles and I would spend an hour washing all the sound cables ready for the next day.

It will be noticed that I have glossed over other jobs in television. I'd like to read of a floor manager's life in the business. Or a designer, videotape engineer or a scene shifter and I bet make-up and hair could raise a few eyebrows!
The production assistant (now termed script supervisor) is the only person to see a show through from absolute start to end with the director. Usually she knew where all the 'bodies were buried'. Exploits of PA's and vision mixers could be a book in themselves. PA's were responsible for looking after the director/producer throughout the formation of a programme or series. Then typing the script and constant amendments then calling the shots from the production gallery on the night. After that, post production where the edit was dictated by the PA's notes, finally the sound dub. From A to Z, PA's ran the gamut.

Today, this job has been decimated and split between many others. ATV had a cacophony of top class PA's. Some left to seek other paths, but they all made their names in both the drama and light entertainment fields

With the freelance world, now getting busier and more populated, it appeared that I had now retired. I didn't advertise it. It was merely that the phone ceased to ring. (Psst! I'm still available for a boom, or whatever!)

In the nineties, the freelance rate wasn't keeping up with inflation and I was loathe to lower my rate. The business was also getting laden with 'runners' anxious to learn everybody's job (and do it for less than considerably less than half the fee). Many runners were the off-spring of directors and producers.

The kids wanted to get into the business and dad got them on a shoot where they could pick up a few tips, see what branch of the business they preferred. And why not? If my dad hadn't looked after my interests, finding me jobs, even attending interviews, I might have been reduced to burring the spark plugs on jam jars.

Now, they'd watch the clapper loader, or the camera tracker or the boom guy and think; *'I can do that, it looks like fun, better than going to work.'*

The advent of women working in television now is astounding. When I started, girls were secretaries, production assistants or vision mixers. The only one sound girl I ever encountered was Patty at the HTV Bristol Studios, although I think Thames Television also broke the mould. Check out a classical concert twenty years ago and see how male dominated it was. Then see the orchestras of today, more women than blokes, even girls playing the trombone or French horn. I recently saw a concert where the percussionist was a young girl – and she was terrific, could have given Buddy Rich a fun for the money.

The same revolution hit the television industry. I am an avid credit watcher, I don't see many names I know now, but am always alerted to the number of ladies in top jobs on the credits. I recollect working on a programme at the Thames-side Riverside Studios where my entire crew were girls. It was the day Ayrton Senna was killed in Formula One.

On *Birds of a Feather*, I was asked to show a young girl the ropes while on a three day location shoot. She took an interest in the job and when I asked her if she wanted to work in sound when she left school, she replied . . .*'Oh no, I'm going to be a producer'* (presumably like her dad?)

I don't think many youngsters have the foggiest what a producer does. Or, to be more precise what they *used* to do. Recently, I saw an episode *of 'Big Little Lies'* with twelve producer credits, all of course, serving different functions. *The Americans* have eight! Every American import now has a cacophony of producer credits. Producer, assistant producer, co-producer and the final irony, three, or more, executive producers. There can only be ONE executive producer. I recently saw an American production boasting no less than six executive producers. Was the title in lieu of dosh?

In Hollywood's heyday and even early television the producer was king. He/she could hire and fire at will. Imagine David O'Selznick, or King Vidor having three other executive producers on their movies? Budgets, staff choice, artiste casting and post production were all in their hands. These days, of course, times have changed. As a result the producer/director role has become blurred.

When I went freelance in 1983, I was probably the only sound director available. Unionism restricted movement and apart from national television there was no other source of work. How things have changed. Now, the BBC and all the commercial companies runs on a skeleton staff with freelance people available if and when required. No more pension schemes for them, if you were sick . . . tough! No show – no dough. Even studio locations have taken a beating .In the Mid-2018, ITV's flagship *Good Morning* programme now comes the BBC T|V Centre.

With the advent of satellite channels and the gigantic digital revolution there are more jobs and many more shows. Not shows like we used to know, the musical extravaganza, the videotaped drama, but fodder for the ever hungry, twenty four hours a day transmitter or that satellite in the Sky.

We are approaching an era where terrestrial television is decreasing at an alarming rate as Netflix, Amazon, All4 and a myriad of other companies lure license payers away via streaming and surfing. More and more people are watching transmissions on their phones or laptops instead of a real television set. One day, someone will ask why we are still paying the BBC a license fee.

Our screens are pack jammed tight with 'real life' documentaries, 'people' shows, knick-knack auctioning, the never-ending house purchase and decoration of, not to mention a cacophony of cooking, how to do this, how to do that, or how NOT to do this or that . . . all eagerly sought by that hungry transmitter or your internet provider.

For the young job hunter; don't be despondent because television companies have shed staff by the bucket load. The industry will continue to expand. There are hundreds of small production companies providing work opportunities. It will always be possible to find employment even starting from scratch.

You will have to have studied the field you prefer. Cameras, sound and engineering will require technical knowledge and *always* display a massive interest – make sure to accentuate this on interview. Occasionally, eagerness can compensate for experience etc. Same rules apply for make-up and hair and all the arms of the industry. Probably the starting pay being offered will be poor but the experience gathered will be worth it. A King's Ransom is probably not at the end of the rainbow but a more interesting life you will have difficulty finding.

But *'what the hay'* even way back before the *Birds of a Feather* period it was time to hang up the headphones and ruminate on the good old days. I remember a TV-AM house magazine advising its readers – if ever you come across any ex-ATV staff whingeing about; *'they don't make shows like we did anymore . . .'* just buy them a pint, keep shtum and let them ramble on before you make your escape.

My career in radio and television has been the result of barrel loads of luck and being fortunate enough to be working for the best TV Company in the world, at just the right time. I have been the luckiest guy ever. Early in my television career, sound people used to be the poor relations of the industry. I can recall a production meeting for a drama where the director was totally engrossed with problems concerning cameras and lighting. He was puzzled why I was there!

However, the advent of the American Specials at ATV, and the innovative sound departments at Thames and London Weekend Television changed that thinking and let us not forget the massive contributions by the Beeb with their great staff of sound guys, following in the footsteps of people like Len Shorey.

I must make a special mention of the London Weekend sound department. They were very innovative in producing an exciting, clean-cut, sharp sound in all their light entertainments programmes. Their pick-up of audience reaction especially was, at times to us, baffling. A recent discussion with ex-LWT people lead me to believe these advances were the result of a sound department able to invest in new thinking and equipment. Something we, at ATV, would have loved to have enjoyed.

My disappointment at giving up the exciting world of sound was greatly lessened by buying a boat in Florida where we spent a couple of great holidays each year and continue to visit on a regular basis.

After my unannounced retirement, I was even considering purchasing a drum kit. This idea was quickly scotched. On refection, something best left to the imagination.

***

I would like to offer my heartfelt thanks to my youngest sister Cindy and her daughter Elizabeth for the work they have put in making the website from which this tome has been enlarge. Cindy (now an American citizen) has lived in Boston, USA for many years now and on various visits my oft-related anecdotes related over many a glass of Rioja (or Californian red) in the marina on Marco Island (Florida's own little Paradise) inspired her to encourage me to put it all on paper;

How the sound guys always got thrashed at ATV playing chess with Tommy Steele. He would walk from boom to boom, make a hasty move and never lose. How Bing Crosby sat in the back of a limo en route to the studio every day, not saying a word to his wife Kathryn (the chauffeur blabbed). How Jimi Hendrix cried on my shoulder in the control room. How Dusty Springfield influenced my view of sound mixing in so many ways.

In 2010 I was nominated for a Lifetime Achievement Award. It originated from Dennis Weinrech, the owner of *VIDEOSONICS*, the famous editing house and later Head of Post Production Sound at Pinewood Studios, responsible for mega hits such as Harry Potter etc.

Dennis also did the introductory speech at a Soho venue where the *UK Screen Sound Awards* would be presented. A dozen, or more, awards went to dubbing mixers and editing houses for big-time feature films. My *Conch* award came towards the end. Needless to say, I was the oldest person there (and the only one wearing a tie!) After the ceremony I got some kindly remarks from fellow winners.

One guy said;

'*Congratulations Ted on the award – and by the way, great shoes'.*

So, thanks a lot Max Bygraves – your advice paid off!

My Conch Award presented by the Head Honcho of Dolby Sound.

You remember I told you about Dwight Hemion winning dozens of awards and not mentioning one? Well, I got this one and, sorry Dwight, I'm shouting it from the rooftops.

***

The Owl logo

This logo appears on the website. The origin is as follows; Great friend and fellow sound director, Bill Nuttall decided on a new life in Australia. Leaving ATV in the late sixties, he took his wife and two young daughters on an epic Volkswagen minibus journey through Europe, Afghanistan, India and all points east towards Perth, where he landed after several months and many adventures. For instance; parking on a beach in Goa for lunch they were invited by the adjacent hotel to use their facilities. They stayed for ten weeks! A very brave family – the Nuttalls.

On one occasion, Bill had to brandish an old (unloaded) service pistol being confronted by a couple of ragged brigands. On arrival at Perth, Bill was offered a job as sound head of sound at a new technical facilities house. It's a pity Bill didn't document those experiences.

Years later, Bill and Dorothy's girls successfully found jobs, one an air stewardess the other pursued a successful career in music (taking after her dad). Eventually, Bill and Dorothy got bored and returned to England in 1984.

Bill and I decided to form a dry hire company renting audio and visual gear and crews. Bill was to be the business brain while I would skivvy and do the occasional shoot. We devised a logo to reflect the company name *Audio-wise;* depicting an owl wearing headphones. The inference being that, despite our combined ages, doing business with us would be a very wise move! A couple of weeks before start-up, Bill tragically and unexpectedly died.

Once again, may I offer my sincere apologies to guys and girls I have inadvertently left out? I never kept a diary thus I can genuinely claim the ravages of time.

Er . . . that's all folks. Take care and remember, a glass of red at night does no harm!!!

***

26. GORDON BENNETT - HOW THE RICH LIVE

If you have enjoyed these ramblings, you might just be interested in my series of GORDON BENNETT ADVENTURES, some of the contents of which will have derived from this account of life in the TV business during the seventies.

Remember my meeting a guy en route from Port Suez to Haifa? We have probably all come across a Gordon Bennett character – well dressed, oozing charm with a constant smile and twinkling eyes. He glides through life with the minimum of effort and seemingly, the maximum of achievement.

Using my Gordon Bennett characters and interweaving their adventures into some telly stuff and figments of my imagination, The HOW THE RICH LIVE trilogy is a light humorous romp through the 1970's with the added bitterness of some sinister undertones.

The theme has little to do with wealth. Many are born rich or inherit rich. Some work hard to be rich . . . then there are others who attained the title *HOW THE RICH LIVE* by methods most wouldn't subscribe to.

The trilogy flips from the UK to Florida then to Spain and back again. It culminates in a success for the bad guys . . . but not for long!

***

Also available in E Book format.

tedscott@ymail.com

Copyright @ 2018 Ted Scott

They can be read separately, although the stories continue from book to book. Even after book three of the trilogy, there's more . . . .

235

Printed in Great Britain
by Amazon